The Ten Minute Quit
© 2018 Margaret Nelson

Front and Back Cover Photo
© 2018 Yakhnenko

With love for my family, near and far.

In gratitude to my parents.

For Eugene.

The Ten Minute Quit:

How I Transitioned to My New Life as a Non-Smoker

First Edition

By
Margaret Nelson

Contents

INTRODUCTION (Don't Skip This!):

Welcome to *The Ten Minute Quit.* Here are some important things you need to know about this book.

What Is This Book About?

This book is a memoir of my experience when I quit smoking cigarettes. I am including insights of my experience. I am also including tips, advice, and directions for anyone who may want to try quitting cigarettes in the same way I did. This book is about me, really just wanting to help anyone who has ever felt alone or misunderstood when they decided to transition to the life of a non-smoker. I wished for a book like this when I quit, and since I couldn't find one at the time, I decided to write one.

Where Does My Credibility Come From?

Let's start by addressing who I actually AM:
I am a human person who was successful in my

journey to quit smoking cigarettes. Actually, I don't smoke anything at all (a necessary disclaimer since I come from California), I don't vape; basically I don't have anything to do with smoking or any type of smoking culture. The authority of my perspective is maintained by these personal views.

I am also a person who has done a lot of research about the ways people learn. At the time of writing this book, I am currently a candidate for a graduate degree in the field of Education. This means I have studied how humans learn things, and how to set up a learner for success. In this book, I have taken this perspective one step alongside my training by viewing myself as the learner, and thinking about how I could facilitate desired habits and behaviors in my own thoughts and actions.

I am also someone who (thankfully) has not been living under a rock. This means I have a lot of natural working knowledge which I would consider as "common knowledge." This common knowledge is something I use a lot in my critical thinking, and has helped develop several strategies in this book, aside from my own personal experience. I include this so you'll know that any similarities to anyone else's strategy is purely coincidence, and likely stems from the same line of thinking around common knowledge.

To sum this up: I am an intelligent human person who is skilled at educational strategies, and used these skills to gain the experience of successfully quitting smoking cigarettes.

Now for who I am NOT:

I am not a medical doctor. I am not a medical anything. Any of my tips and/or advice are to be used at your own risk, and are never intended to replace the qualified opinion of a medical professional. This includes professionals in the field of medicine, psychiatry, and natural or developed wellness professions.

Man. I always feel cranky when I write disclaimers. You've got the idea though, right? This is my book about my experience, and it's not going to replace a visit to the doctor's office, Ok? So, do try this at home...if you want to, and at your own risk.

Can we get to the happy, fun, quit stuff now?
Great! Ready-Set-Go!!!!

Scared To Start, Part 1: Identity Crisis

Some Backstory:

It was the end of my regular check-up, and my doctor was being kind. I had always noticed my heartbeat was irregular, especially as an adult. All my life, every doctor who had ever listened to it seemed to think was nothing to worry about, so I didn't worry about it either. This time was different.

I felt that of course, this doctor couldn't outright say I was in the "danger zone," not that I needed her to. Imagine your doctor putting her stethoscope to your chest, and the first word she says is "Uh,...Margaret?" Uneven as it was, that made my clumsy little heart wibble-wobble even faster.

The gist of the doctor's explanation was that although it may not have been extreme when I was younger, my heartbeat had clearly progressed to the point where it was time to check it out. She hinted that it was not only for my overall health, but that my heartbeat indicated a situation that could unexpectedly prove disastrous...perhaps even fatal.

I thought about my grandfather, who had a pacemaker for the last several years of his life. I thought about my current schedule participating in management school, working full-time, not getting sleep, not being able to eat regular meals (much less healthy ones). Why had I--and all my previous doctors--overlooked this part of my family history? How had I come so far with having forgotten these factors, while simultaneously not paying attention to my current lifestyle? Wasn't it possible that my heart was blaring an alarm with each stumbling, lopsided beat? On further reflection of my health history, I realized I wasn't sure which had come first: the irregular heartbeat, or the debilitating panic attacks that had come without warning since my childhood?

My point is, here was a situation where I'd had no answers. I felt a little betrayed by the authority figures in my life who had been just as blind as I was now, even when I was only a child who hadn't known better.

Making a Decision From The Heart:

We all get these sort of "crossroad" moments in our lives. At this time, I was presented with a choice to make. On one hand, I could take my chances, writing this experience off as "no big deal," and to convince myself I was simply being too sensitive. My other choice was listening to my doctor, and to accept that sometimes God gives us a warning, maybe even several, and we can choose to listen to it this time, or talk about it more in heaven. This wasn't a paint color, or even a college major we were talking about here. My heart was at stake. My one-of-a-kind, literally-once-in-a-lifetime beating heart. It was too important to ignore any longer. I picked the second choice.

Of course, this meant several changes in my lifestyle were in order. No caffeine (a challenge for a former barista), purposeful cardio exercise, stress management, and as much avoidance of toxicity as I could muster. This meant no more junk food, sure. But I knew, also, that this had to, had to, had to mean (as much as I hated it, that smoking cigarettes was now and forever completely out of the question.

Oh, how I completely and utterly loathed this idea. I knew it was right. Still hated it. I knew it could save my life, and STILL seethed with burning hatred at this idea. On an intellectual level, I could cope with the idea of having to lose a bad habit. I could intellectually handle the idea that there is an adjustment period involved when changing habits. It is, after all, simple logical thinking: Changing a habit is hard. Duh. I think even kindergarteners know that (and sometimes people give them stickers as a reward). I could rationally search tools for help and for information. Nowadays, there's an app for everything.

Emotionally, I was not so "well adjusted," shall-we-say. I was amazed at the emotions I was experiencing: Shock, betrayal by my body, betrayal by the world for not being a world which could just let me smoke when I wanted and have nothing bad at all ever happen from it, indignation, and fear. Fear! Fear of how I would have to live. Fear of who I would be. Anger at being expected to suddenly be an entirely different person, I mean how DARE the world be asking this of me?!

Uh, 'Scuse Me?

That whole temper tantrum is what gave me pause. I had a whole lifestyle to rebuild, but for some reason, quitting smoking was the only thing that sent me into an emotional tailspin. I was ONLY just talking about quitting smoking cigarettes. Why in the world did that suddenly mean I had to be a completely different human being?

"Who would I be without cigarettes?" Was that *seriously* a question I had just asked myself?

Why were my instincts telling me that I would be a completely different person without cigarettes? What did that say about cigarettes and what they were doing to my own sense of identity?

That's when it struck me, how truly insidious addictions are. Cigarettes had slowly, puff by puff and year by year, built a film over my self-awareness, and I hadn't even noticed it happening. It had become such that I literally could not examine myself without seeing through this film. I did not have any self-awareness that didn't pass this vision through cigarettes first.

They had taken over my identity.

I didn't know what was going to happen. All I knew was that this time, win or lose, I was going to fight back.

Scared To Start, Part 2: Those Big, Bad Cravings

There is a sort of stigma that cigarette smokers are lazy, irresponsible, and uncaring. This is most often completely untrue. The majority of cigarette smokers whom I have known are all people I would describe as: caring, empathetic, responsible, loving, driven, disciplined, over-worked, and critical thinkers.

Nicotine is a Stimulant

One of the most powerful things I learned during my quit is that nicotine is a powerful, powerful STIMULANT. Not only is it a powerful stimulant, I read about it being one of *the most powerful* stimulant substances known today! I have even heard of doctors comparing it to cocaine.

Behind the Smoky Stimulant Curtain:

Cigarettes are well-known as a "trick" for models to manage their weight, though it sounds like something from a black and white television show. I would very readily believe that this is something that is still true today. Nicotine revs you up, and suddenly you can get tons more work done without having to stop and eat. The problem is, of course, not all of your calories go to your stomach. A considerable amount of our nutrition is strictly for our brains. Yes, your brain actually needs calories just to do its brain-thing. Any wonder why those "Miss America" question and answer sessions can get so very "out there?"

With nicotine being such a powerful stimulant, is it any wonder that cigarettes can trick the body into believing it isn't hungry? Now, I am not going to go into a conspiracy discussion about how we may live in a land which has some "powers-that-be" who are perfectly satisfied with allowing us access to as much mind-numbing substances as we please (some of which are now legal in California). After all, we all simply want world peace, do we not? I'm just asking if we are so very surprised that we live in a country that allows a stimulant which convinces our bodies that we don't need that nutrition. The working middle class--often denied proper rest breaks and downtime--doesn't miss it if they don't feel their own natural need for nutrition and health. I'm in this class, I totally get what it feels like to work until I drop, especially for fear of losing my job if my employer doesn't constantly observe me giving more of myself than I actually have. I don't wonder at all about the fact that this is the part of the population whom I have noticed smoking the most. I get it: not having to stop and eat means we can keep on working without interruption. We might even get a mood boost, so we are going all day without replenishing ourselves, and we can actually seem *happy about it!*

Cigarettes also stimulate our other systems as well. I know many cigarette smokers who rely on cigarettes to--ahem--get things going in the bathroom in the mornings, if you catch my drift. When I quit, I learned about how the systems that regulate the efficiency of my intestines come to rely on the stimulation provided by nicotine. Over time, they "forget" how to do things without nicotine, and things can become a little backed-up for a while.

This can mean discomfort, sure. But what I thought about more is the way inefficient intestines means our bodies can't absorb nutrition as effectively. Common sense, right? We all feel slightly panicked when we are very hungry. That's just human instinct for the body to say "Mayday! Find a protein source or eat some tree bark, quick! Something, anything!" How might you feel if your body felt that way all the time? You'd panic at the idea of needing nutrition all the time. For the nicotine addict, the instinctive reaction is a fear of inadequate nutrition. Imagine having your arms and legs cut off, and then being left in the wild to fend for yourself. How in the world are you supposed to survive in the wild without arms or legs? Of course, we can survive without nicotine.

My point is that the digestive system becomes dependent on nicotine to get it going, and keep it going. The idea of being without it can, I believe, create an instinctive reaction for the body that makes us literally fear for our own survival in that moment. What's even worse, the suffering of hunger is something we have trained ourselves to cope with using--you guessed it--cigarettes to suppress our appetites.

That's the physical side of things. As I mentioned a little bit before, nicotine also stimulates us emotionally. I'm sure we all know cigarette smokers who light up a cigarette when they are feeling stressed. Pay closer attention, and you'll see them light up when they are happy as well. 100% of us. Sad? There they go. Embarrassed? Puff away. It's not so much that nicotine stimulates us when we are feelings stressed. Nicotine stimulates us when we feel *anything,* because **nicotine is a stimulant.** Just like our physical systems, after a while our emotional lives become dependent on nicotine as well.

It's as though we forget how to process our emotions without nicotine giving us that chemical nudge to propel us forward. Some of us started smoking as older teenages, which means that regardless of our intelligence, we *never* got to learn how to process emotions using only an adult brain. Forget the Miss America answers, this totally explains some of the all-out ridiculous things people say on the street sometimes!

Even though it's hard sometimes, doesn't it still make more sense to have mercy towards people who smoke cigarettes, no matter how or why they got started? Morality aside, I believe it's worth a second look at people who suffer with conditions that mean literally all their biological and mental processes have been trained to operate with nicotine first.

No wonder the idea of being without nicotine can seem so intimidating at first. No wonder the idea of cravings can be so scary sometimes.

Changing the Rules on "Cravings"

Don't you find it interesting that smoking cessation products use the word "cravings?" This product reduces cravings. That product makes cravings manageable. This pill eliminates cravings altogether.

From now on, we are going to forever use a different word for that feeling we get when our body unwittingly asks for more nicotine. We need to stop using the term "cigarette cravings."

Smoking cessation products are helpful, don't get me wrong. I myself utilized them during the first three weeks of my quit. But let's face facts: these products are made by companies. These companies are companies so that they can make money. They only make their money so long as you keep buying their products.

I believe this is why those products all use the word "Cravings." We don't have cigarette cravings. We simply don't.

Cravings are for pregnant women. Cravings can suggest what a body needs in order to support a growing baby, or to suggest how the levels of hormones are balancing, again while a body is supporting a growing baby. The body relies on the stored information from a lifetime of eating experiences to ask specifically for the source that will give the body what it needs (which is another argument in favor of a diet consistently including fruits and veggies, but that's another book). Cravings are rewarded by the body with feelings of happiness and satisfaction. Cravings make life interesting. Cravings give our brain things to look forward to.

Cravings are for things we need for happy, healthy, biologically successful lives--including the lives of those who aren't born yet.

BUT, no one has ever, in the history of the human race, actually needed nicotine.

This is why smoking cessation products should be used with care. They are helpful to some people to be sure, but they are not to be blindly trusted. After all, they use the word "cravings," which means they know full well that they are back-handedly supporting a continued addiction to nicotine. They want you to subconsciously *continue wanting nicotine.* They want you to keep feeling as though nicotine is a biological *need.* In this way, you will keep having to quit. In this way, you will keep having to go back to buy more of their products.

Again, I stress: These products are really helpful to some people, myself included! But they are only effective at doing what they *say* they are going to do so long as they help you quit, and help keep you quit. With the right help to back you up, and the right kinds of changes outlined in this book, there's no telling how fast and fully you can succeed!

Returning to these so-called "cravings," let's discuss what they really are, instead of the lie fed to us by consumerism.

I propose that from now on, we throw out the word "cravings," and instead use the word "withdrawal," since that's exactly what we're dealing with.

What Nicotine Withdrawal Feels Like:
Feel free to show this to Non-Smokers so that they can learn more about what you are going through!

1. Waves of withdrawal are extremely disorienting at first. I didn't exactly feel dizzy, but there were times during those first few days when I felt like I didn't have an awareness of the space around me the way I usually did. It was alarming until I realized it was just a withdrawal.

2. The entire body feels awkward at first. I suddenly didn't feel comfortable sitting, or standing. I suddenly had no idea what to do with my hands. I didn't know where in the rom I wanted to be. Breathing changed from involuntary to being awkward and uneven for a few moments.

3. They can make you feel vulnerable at first. Because at that moment I was not secure in my body or in the space around my body, my stress response was triggered in a huge way. I could have jumped at the slightest sound. Any insensitive comments in this moment would have hit me a million times harder than normal. I had no secure barrier to let me instinctively know where I stopped

and the rest of the world began. I felt incredibly exposed during those moments.

4. They make you feel obvious. I'm sure there were moments when it would have been hard to tell what was wrong with me.I'm sure there were times when I seemed normal. I have to take this on faith, however, because it sure didn't feel this way to me at the time. Withdrawal symptoms left me feeling as though everyone could see what I was going through. I felt that I might as well have been having a public temper tantrum on the floor. I felt like I might as well have been shouting "I WANT NICOTINE" at the top of my lungs--that's how conspicuous and obvious I felt. It felt a little shameful, and pretty embarrassing, which compounded the pressure I was already under. I remember wishing at that moment that someone could have reassured me that I didn't look like a monster, even if I did feel like one inside.

5. They can make you feel like a toddler who needs a time-out. Seriously, I am not kidding about the temper tantrums. Not only was I irritable from the fight-or-flight reflex, I had no clear action to take to work through it because my whole body felt awkward and immovable. Now add to the mix that

withdrawals also happen while we SLEEP! For me, this resulted in some truly bizarre dreams which prevented any deep, recuperative sleep. There are two days in my memory when I was so overwhelmed by this potion of symptoms, the only thing I could do was sit and cry about it, and that's exactly what I did. I cried like a toddler might cry after falling down. Praise God: this really did help.

These are nicotine withdrawals in a nutshell. They are not "quit" symptoms. Just take a moment to think about that. They don't magically happen only when you decide to leave cigarettes forever. *This process starts the moment we extinguish a cigarette, any cigarette, EVERY CIGARETTE!* It's pretty common knowledge nowadays that nicotine only stays in our systems a short while before withdrawals start to kick in. I've read this happens in as quickly as 20 minutes after extinguishing a cigarette! Think about how you have been battling these withdrawal symptoms while also miraculously functioning in your life. It is nothing short of championship, the way we can work through this and also be effective in our jobs, be loving family members, be generous caretakers, and have the mental strength to actually dream about better lives for ourselves. Seriously: We all deserve a pat on the back.

Look over the list of symptoms I experienced again, and think about which ones you might relate to, if you have ever quit cigarettes before. Can you believe how much you have endured? I challenge anyone who is judgemental toward cigarette smokers to look that over, and to think about how well they might do if *they* went through that every 20 minutes! Why would they want anyone to go through that?

Then again, why would we want to keep putting ourselves through that? Especially if there really truly is a way out? What if we could be free of this cycle?

Before I quit smoking cigarettes, I realized this about withdrawals: If this withdrawal process has begun every time I put out a cigarette, then it is very likely that the only way to be free of them forever is never to smoke. Lighting up a cigarette again certainly relieved them for the time-being, but *smoking only ever reset the clock back to the beginning of my withdrawal symptoms.* As long as I smoked, I would certainly have to go through them all again. As much as I hated to face the facts on this, the only way OUT of them was THROUGH.

This is also how I learned that there is no such thing as smoking one cigarette. The "social smoker" concept is a complete and total myth. I guarantee anyone who calls themselves a "social smoker" may be kidding themselves by saying they only smoke around other people. They may be so desperate to hang on to this delusion that they even become angry at the idea that they could actually be hooked. Go ahead and watch them, and you'll see people who find more and more excuses to be around people who smoke, just so that they can smoke. The end game there is not to socialize. It's getting to smoke a cigarette. Soon they'll be back to smoking cigarettes alone, just like you and I did. It can happen to any of us. For some of us, that's exactly how it happened!

None of us are immune. That's why I feel it is so important to hold ourselves accountable AND to encourage each other. We all know what it's like to battle these nicotine withdrawals. I believe that somewhere inside of us all, we know that these withdrawals can be survived. It is truly possible to come out on the other side of them, with the right mindset, the right tools, and a great plan. Freedom is real. It can happen.

We don't have to do this alone.

Your "New" Identity

So far, we've covered how cigarettes invade our understanding and awareness of who we are. We have also talked about how this problem is complicated (at least it was for me) by the fact that we can't really rely on how we feel--not, at least, when all of our biological processes have been conditioned to defer first to nicotine on physical, emotional, and psychological levels.

In short, it's awfully difficult to know which parts of you are truly you, and which parts have been enslaved by an addiction to nicotine.

When I came to this realization, I observed that what this nicotine addiction had done to my self-esteem is very similar to the results abusive relationships create within the senses of self and self-worth of their victims. In an abusive relationship, the victim must defer to the unpredictable and damaging moods of the abuser in order to have the best chances for continual survival, as unscathed as possible. I was both consciously and subconsciously obsessed with my sources of nicotine, and every action in my life had to ensure that this drive, this "need," was met first and foremost before my actual, authentic needs.

That sums up a pretty darn abusive relationship, if you ask me.

It's pretty common knowledge nowadays that people who stay in abusive relationships often do so for fear of their safety, or for the safety of their loved ones. In an abusive relationship, the most danger occurs right after the time of leaving that relationship, and not all are successful in their escape attempts. What I would like to point out is that nicotine addiction feels very much the same. We have already covered a little bit about the way all the physical, emotional, and psychological processes become dependent on using nicotine to keep them going. To simply leave a relationship with nicotine *feels* just as dangerous as leaving an abusive relationship. All our instincts, all our biology, all our emotions, all our experiences all point to the need of nicotine for survival.

Here is some very good news for you: All of those feelings are a BIG FAT LIE.

We absolutely do NOT need nicotine for survival. I say this multiple times in this book because while your body experiences withdrawal, I hope you'll remember my encouragement as a friend: Your body might make you feel like you need nicotine to survive, but you don't. You are going to live! Not only this, but during the course of this book, you are going to develop strategies to thrive in your new life as a non-smoker! Hang in there!

I know this side of the process seems daunting. It is really helpful to keep our minds on the problem: How do we combat this chemical abuser of us, which has taken over all our processes to the point that we don't even know which parts of ourselves do NOT contain it's influence?

Here's how I propose we accomplish this:

We build our senses of self.

We focus on self care.

We take a mini-break from complicated philosophical questions ("Where do I fit in the world?," "What is my life's purpose?,") and instead we just commit to a couple weeks of simply living each day very very well.

We focus on where we fit in our own skin.

We know we've been in here all along, behind the smokescreen.

We choose to fight for ourselves.

We remember the people that love us likely are able to see us for who we are, not just our nicotine addiction. We allow ourselves to feel grateful for having these people in our lives.

We decide to leave this abusive situation.

We commit to it, no matter what: no matter about the fact that our body is going to think we are in mortal danger, until our biological systems re-learn what life is like without nicotine.

We commit to it, even if we feel like it'll take multiple attempts. Failure isn't really failure if we learn from it and use it to create a better strategy for next time.

These are the things I thought about when I realized I was finally ready to quit. Shortly after, the most amazing thing happened. My soul was suddenly flooded with feelings of empathy, love, peace, patience, and goodness. I suddenly had more of these things in my heart than ever before. Not just on behalf of myself, either. I felt love, empathy, and mercy for all of us, for all my fellow human beings, and I also knew at that time that I would be writing this book. I knew I had to be successful in quitting so that I could write about it for anyone who might find it helpful. I had the desire to be an encourager, a good neighbor, and a friend to all who needed to take the same paths that I did.

I think ultimately what finally happened was that I was able to give this kind of love to *myself,* for exactly who and how I was, *in that moment.* We all need a little love, don't we? Growing and accepting these feelings within myself allowed me to give myself some much-needed love, and this in turn allowed me to extend that love to others. It's like that old saying: You can't give what you don't have. Once I gave myself love and validation, and accepted myself as a human being, I was able to do that for other people. I sincerely hope you will too.

I knew then that I wanted to tell you:

You are not your nicotine addiction. You are so much more.

You are NOT wrong, bad, weak, lazy, or dumb because you are addicted to nicotine.

There is a life that is free from the shame surrounding nicotine addiction.

It is possible for you to have that life. It really, truly is.

You don't have to do this alone. You shouldn't do this alone. Don't be alone.

When you are free from your nicotine addiction, you will not have some "new" identity. Nicotine has been covering up your identity, not changing it. There is a wonderful, beautiful, worthy, good person inside of you, and I don't want you to give up on giving that person a beautiful life.

In this book, I am going to explain how I built up my "new" sense of self, and got myself back to living like the person I was always meant to be. I hope that it helps you become inspired to do the same for yourself. You can borrow my strategies and choices until you come up with some approaches of your own. Mine are all written down for you in this book, easily browseable, affordable, fast, and most importantly, they are all positive ways to have a better day, withdrawal or not.

It's going to be ok. Everything is going to be alright.

It's time to see yourself again, and to get rid of the toxic smokescreen covering up your identity--literally.

It's time to let some good sunshine in your life.

You can do this.

Good Friends, Bad Friends

Quitting smoking is a healing process. I don't believe it takes a lifetime to quit, but you won't be out of the woods by this time next week, either. As far as this process goes, my experience makes me feel pretty confident in saying that when you quit, you're likely going to need to settle into it for a little while. It's a process, and all your systems need a reboot.

Since this is likely going to be a (perhaps small but still significant) period of your life, it's important to have as good a support system as you can muster.

The rule for finding these types of supportive relationships is pretty simple: Imagine you are going through a tough breakup. Which people, or which types of people, are you likely to reach out for comfort and/or common sense? If you were going through a breakup, would you enjoy being around people who are in relationships that remind you of the one you don't have anymore? If you were going through a breakup, would you enjoy being around people who understand you? What about people who could listen to you complain about your ex (for a little while) or could give you some good confidence-boosting pep talks? What about people who simply sat and listened? What about people who would introduce you to new people, things, or to other ways you could be using your newfound available time?

A relationship with nicotine is a little bit different, however. It's important to remember that any relationship with nicotine is an abusive one. That's right--even if you have tapered-down to just two cigarettes a day, or if you only smoke one cigarette in a month, you are in an abusive relationship with nicotine. ANY relationship with nicotine is an abusive one. Sooner or later, just like abusive human relationships, you are going to have to go No Contact. Just take a deep breath and recognize that fact right now, because if you decide to quit, you must accept that No Contact day is coming. Don't be afraid. This is good, it is necessary, and it is right. By the end of this book, you are going to have an EXACT idea of tons of things you can do with your time instead of spending it with nicotine. It's going to be alright.

It makes sense to think of this nicotine quit as a breakup with a villainous, abusive partner for whom you have developed a significant emotional and physical attachment. No, not attachment: *obsession.*

Here are some great personalities to look for as you build your Quit Team. These people are great to have on your side as allies while your mind, body, and spirit do some much-deserved healing.

Nicotine Breakup Buddies

The Good Shoulder Angel:

This person is your shoulder to cry on during the first stages of your quit when your entire body and soul feel just downright awkward. This person should be in the circle of your most trusted people, and should not be afraid to see you behaving like a toddler. Trust me, you'll feel like a toddler at *least* once or twice during this process (and that's ok). Bonus points too, if this person is also able to help you decide on amounts of time you'll spend grieving. They might say something like: "Let's grieve about this for

10 minutes, and then we're going to go get a glass of water."

The Angel Who Always Knew You Could:

In my opinion, one of the best things a person can say to a cigarette smoker goes a little something like: "I know you can quit when you're ready, and when you are ready to try it out, I will be there to help you." This person may not agree with your choices, but the fact that they can tell you so kindly means that this person is likely both reliable and loving--things we really need during times of recovery and change. If you are a cigarette smoker, it is perfectly acceptable to say this to yourself, too. Say it to your reflection, often and sincerely.

The Voice-of-Reason Angel:

Just like it is when leaving an abusive relationship, there will likely be a point when you feel like going back to your nicotine addiction. Eventually, you'll be able to reason with yourself and overcome that temptation, but it takes practice, and you might just fail at it a few times. Keep trying. While you are getting that practice in, I think it's smart to have a peer who can tell you not to go back. This is not an excuse for your friend to be a jerk and boss you around. This is a peer who can remind you of what you have accomplished. If you are reading this as someone helping a friend or loved one quit, here are some helpful phrases to be the angel your loved one needs right now:

"I know you're thinking about giving up, but since that's such a big decision, let's see if you still feel the same way tomorrow/in an hour/in ten minutes."

"Don't decide to smoke again until after you have drunk this entire bottle of water."

"Don't decide to smoke again until after you've had a snack."

"Don't decide to smoke again until after you've had a walk."

"Don't decide to smoke again until after you have resolved this problem at work."

Again, the Voice-of-Reason Angel is a voice of reason, not a voice of judgement. This person should also be prepared for your tears when you have a meltdown after accepting the reality that you really just can't get away with smoking anymore, ever.

The Angel Who is Fun to Walk With:

Walking was a huge part of my life during the first few weeks of my quit. Especially while the nicotine was still in my system, my nervous system was stimulated all the time, and I had to burn off that extra energy in order to avoid feelings of panic. The type of buddy that will be a real angel to you here is the kind of person who is fun to walk with. You'll be engaged in the activity, you'll detox by sweating, and you'll feel mentally and emotionally rewarded by time outside and connection to another living being. This type of buddy is simply willing to go walking with you. It's also great if they are able to tell you how their day is going. This will help you get your mind off of yourself and your work for a moment, which will also likely be refreshing and restorative. If you don't have a friend to walk with, walk your dog! If you don't have a dog, seriously: GET. A. DOG.

The Angel Who Has Done It:

This person has quit smoking, has come out on the other side, and truly enjoys his/her new life as a non-smoker. This person has learned some great coping skills. This person is also ready, willing, and able to share tons of personal experience in a way that is *for you,* in support of *you,* without needing *you* to do anything except use what might be helpful to you during this time. I had a little trouble finding this person. Sure, I knew people who had quit before, but they wanted to talk about their personal experiences because they needed me to validate their hard work--they weren't trying to lighten the load for me or anyone else. Since I had a little trouble finding this person, I decided to be this person, and to write this book for anyone else struggling to find someone like this.

These are just a few of the personalities you might find to be truly wonderful allies to you while you quit smoking cigarettes. I want to take this opportunity to remind you that your friends are like everything else in your life at this time: You're going to have to consciously decide to seek the good, and you're going to have to consciously decide to avoid any elements or people that are unhelpful or unproductive to you goal.

That being said, it's important to cover the personalities which I feel ought to be avoided as much as possible, at least during this recovery time. These people likely mean very well, but their own levels of emotional maturity are going to just add white noise on top of an already over-stimulating situation. They aren't evil by any means, just misguided, misinformed, and perhaps a little immature. Here are some of the people I would actively avoid while recovering:

Nicotine Breakup Dummies

The Dummy On the Street:

...Or anybody who has ever shamed you about smoking. I can't tell you how many times strange men told me I was "too pretty to smoke." Nevermind that I could get cancer, and my quality of life is in the pits, which affected my sense of self and self-worth, but as long as I stay pretty, it's all fine and good with you, Sir? It's a jerk guy thing to do this. Seriously: I think it's a way to further demean someone else's sense of self-worth by saying the only thing that qualifies them being worthwhile is whether or not they are physically attractive, and the worst part is that this is disguised (poorly) as somehow caring for their fellow human beings. Creep-o's. Also: Special shout-out to the old ladies who publicly shamed me or a friend for smoking by doing the cough-plus-dirty-look move, or saying to my non-smoking friend (or to me when I became the non-smoker) that the smoking party is "not worth it," is "no good," or any other variation of that. I'm not kidding--real live people actually did this! They also followed-up with the instruction to "dump/forget/get rid of him/her." All I can say to them is: Why thank you, random stranger, for giving me your totally useful (not) judgement on my life right now! It is truly most effective to hear your unsolicited advice and condescension. In fact, I think I just quit smoking! You, random stranger, are a miracle worker! I'm cured!

I can usually resist sarcasm, but as you can see,

this is still an area where sarcasm just comes way too easily to me.

The best I can figure is that it must be a lot easier to quit smoking cigarettes than it is to decide not to be a jerk. While you are recovering, I hereby give you full permission to mentally give the finger to anyone who decides to publicly shame you. Better yet, nothing works quite as well as the truth combined with personal boundaries. Consider asserting yourself and your right to live by using some variation of these phrases:

"You are a complete stranger and I don't care what you think."

"You do not have my permission to approach me. Go away."

"I don't like you right now."

"I want you to stop talking to me right now."

"You are acting like a real big jerk."

If you do use one of these phrases, you should be

warned that people do not like to be caught misbehaving. You may get some defensive retaliation, but that happens whenever we set a personal boundary with people who do not respect the boundaries of others. It shouldn't matter if they begin to retaliate, because you'll have already started walking away by this time, right? RIGHT? Seriously. Walk away.

Being assertive is not the same as being aggressive. Remember that you are a human PERSON. You get to say what you will and will not tolerate from others. Period. You have every right to remove yourself from a situation that impedes your personal boundaries. And as your friend and neighbor on this, I *expect you to remove yourself from as much toxicity as possible.*

The Dummy Who Makes You Promise:

This dummy isn't actually a jerk. He or she is likely someone who truly cares for you, and probably even loves you dearly. Plus side: This person likely just wants you to be happy and healthy, and to have a good life. Downside: This person obviously has had little to no training in how to handle emotions, relationships, stress, change, anything really. This category also includes people who threaten to remove you from their last will and testament, people who tell you they'll come visit your house only after you quit, and basically any other way people might manipulate you into committing to quit smoking cigarettes before you decide you're ready. Let's not forget the folks who have placed such emotional significance in *their* lives for *you* quitting, they are likely going to burst into tears upon the sight of your lighter. They'll say, "You P-p-p-promised!"

Like I said before, the intention is likely rooted in a place of truly real love and caring, and whenever possible, I am fully in support of reacting with patience, love, and calm. I simply find the approach to be manipulative, because you'd have to quit in order to meet *their* satisfaction. For one thing, it'll never work. You have to quit for you, out of love of your own life. For another, you'll secretly resent these people for manipulating you when you're suffering already. News flash: BEING ADDICTED TO ANYTHING IS NOT FUN! Finally, this is your recovery time, not theirs, or anyone else's. Your one and only job right now is to make sure you are getting support for the new life you are creating. If you aren't getting support, the very least people can do is get out of the way and avoid putting pressures on you that make the job of recovery even an ounce heavier than is necessary. Don't worry. If these people are so very attached to you quitting, they'll forgive you for the temporary break in the closeness of your relationship while you recover. They'll likely be especially overjoyed when you return to them as an accomplished non-smoker! Maybe they'll even throw you a party!

The Fake Buddy Dummy:

This is a person who pretends to be a friend to you during this time. This person has all kinds of backhanded ways to get on your case about smoking cigarettes. I've had coworkers launch right into their anti-tobacco speeches before so much as a "Good Morning." How about the "friend" who gives you a beautifully-wrapped birthday present with smoking cessation pamphlets or products inside? "Happy Birthday! This is because I want you to live long enough to have another birthday! Loooooove!" Yeah….that's laughably unhelpful.

It's time to cut any toxicity or inauthenticity from your life. If you need someone to officially give you permission for this, look no further: As your friend, I officially give you permission to just simply not talk to these kinds of dummies during your recovery (or ever again, if that's what you wind up choosing). Seriously, for the next six months, just pretend they died on Mars, or something. Your self-esteem will thank you, and your sense of self-worth will have an even better chance of blossoming during your recovery period.

The Dummies Who Don't Even Try to Pretend:

To support you, that is. This includes the category of people who point out that you need a plan for dealing with your new non-smoker weight, for example. Also included are current smokers who simply cannot deal with your quit plan, because it makes them feel too guilty for not having one of their own yet.

Conversations with these people probably start off with you being excited about some aspect of your quit plan, and making the mistake of mentioning it to them. Then, as though it has been rehearsed, you'll hear them launch into all the reasons they started smoking in the first place, why they love smoking, and all the reasons why it "simply isn't the right time" for them to quit. Well, who mentioned THEIR quit? You were talking about YOURS! Believe me, you're going to come across more people like this than you ever thought was possible.

It's great to have people around you with different perspectives. Diversity is valuable, truly! My point here, however, is that this is your path. This recovery belongs to no one else but you, and this is going to require that you make decisions which will feel selfish at first. To this I can only say that self-care is self-ish. And necessary. This category of dummies isn't full of enemies, not by a long shot. However, it is full of people who, for some understandable and very good reasons, simply don't have it in them to support you at this time. You'll want them to be happy for you, but they will simply never be mentally capable of that. You've been warned. Love them, and keep moving on with your plan.

The Worst Kind of Dummy:

This is anyone, ever, for any reason, in any situation, who makes you feel somehow less interesting or attractive after quitting. Yes, that includes anyone who has negative things to say about any weight you may have gained as a non-smoker. By that time, you will have quit smoking cigarettes, you will have asserted yourself as the master over your nicotine addiction, and by God: Anyone who is willing to work as hard, sweat as much, and put as much on the line as you have in order to accomplish this is certainly welcome to conversation as a PEER. Even so, no one EVER has the right to make you feel badly about any weight you may have gained on the journey through your nicotine addiction. No one ever has the right to make you feel badly for needing to sit somewhere else while the group is smoking, or for needing to be where you aren't getting smoke blown into your face. It's unacceptable. Period. This is another situation where the psychic middle finger is a-ok, in my book.

Rate Your Circle:

Take a second and think about all these different personality types, both helpful and unhelpful. Based on your reflections, who do you want to remain in your life right now? Who remains in your inner circle, and who is going to get a friendship "time out" during your recovery? Write their names below.

I want these people to remain in my life during my recovery from smoking cigarettes:

_____

_____

I am comfortable with these people having intimate working knowledge of my progress during my recovery:

_____

_____

For whatever reason, although they will remain in my life, these people seem to simply not be capable of giving me the support and encouragement I need during my recovery process:

_____

_____

These relationships are toxic to me because they are bad influences, or simply do not inspire/motivate me to be a better me:

_____

_____

If a person is a bad influence, here's some advice: *don't go around them anymore.* If a person does not inspire or motivate you somehow to make better choices for yourself, then they are not on your team. Avoid at all costs.

Your Dream Team:

I hope this chapter has given you some good insight into the influences that surround you. It is possible you have discovered some influences who perhaps let you to cigarettes, or have been keeping you close to cigarettes. It's time to let these influences go.

Remember: You have every right to your recovery. You do not have to wait for someone else to believe that you deserve to feel better. You get to say when it is time for you to start feeling better. You get to say when it is time for you to start *being* better.

Final Note:

I probably don't have to tell you, but this is written from the assumption that you are still being as considerate as possible as a cigarette smoker. Don't smoke around infants or the elderly, or anyone you know who has breathing issues, or near the entrances of buildings. Don't smoke around impressionable people, like children. Don't smoke obnoxious-smelling things out in public. Don't blow smoke at people. Be nice to people, so that you're justified in wanting them to be nice to you.

It Only Takes Ten Minutes

Boy do I ever have some good news for you.

If you're anything like me, you'll be looking at the beginning of your quit the same way someone might look through a loooooong tunnel. It seems so very far to the other side. The pressure of the oncoming darkness can seem suffocating and/or impossible. But it isn't. True, I wish we could take the entire journey in one single bound. How easy that would be! Then it would be over, bada-bing, bada-boom, and we could go on to our next life adventure! We both know that isn't the way it works. There are real big transitions ahead, and you are going to experience some withdrawal symptoms.

The Good News About Withdrawal Symptoms:

The withdrawal symptoms only happen part of the time, not all of the time. You will not be barraged by symptoms every second of every day. There are tons of breaks in-between them. The breaks will seem short at first, even if they aren't, but incredible soon, they'll start becoming longer and longer. You're going to get breaks long enough to catch your breath (literally!), watch a movie, spend time with your spouse, enjoy a sunset, cook a meal, or even fall asleep for a comfortable nap.

I even have good news about the withdrawals themselves! While they are intense at first, it is important to remember that the body likes consistency, and will naturally try to build habits. Each wave of withdrawal symptoms you experience can actually help your body to reset, and it really truly does become accustomed to them. That means that each wave of withdrawal you endure should feel less and less intense. I noticed considerably lighter withdrawal waves within the first few days. Now that I have been a non-smoker for a couple years, I am not bothered by them at all. Does my brain still ask for nicotine? Occasionally. But it's more of a passing feeling, a remembrance of the way things used to be, than it is of a request or a face craving. It doesn't tempt, hurt, or irritate me one bit. This is also why I can be around current cigarette smokers, and enjoy their company with zero discomfort.

"Will they ever go away completely?" I get asked that a lot. My view is this:

I don't think you're scared of having withdrawals. You had withdrawals as a smoker, every single time you put out a cigarette, and it didn't bother you. You are not scared of withdrawals. You are likely just scared that withdrawals will make you suffer. So do they ever go away? Hey man, I don't know. Smoking cigarettes is something that changes your life. But you know what? So does staying out in the sun too long. It can be harmful, right? So if you get a freckle from the sun, it changes your body forever, true. Your body now has a freckle where there wasn't one before. But do freckles hurt? Not normally! My point is that it's reasonable for your brain to always remember what smoking is like, and when it would resort to a nicotine fix. It'll always remember the cues to smoke. BUT, it will not always cause you anxiety or irritation.

...and if your freckles hurt, it's probably doctor time for you. Just bein' a friendly neighbor.

Why Ten Minutes At A Time is Best:

There are tons of programs that promote change and self-growth, using each day as an opportunity for a fresh start. I really think this is great to keep in mind, because my opinion is that this is true! Each day really is an opportunity for a fresh start.

All the same, when I first started on my quit, whole days felt like eons. Nicotine addiction really does some awful things to those willpower muscles. I felt like I could never get through a whole day. I started to dread mornings, because I saw them as the beginning of a monumental task which I felt I could never achieve. This always made me feel so very guilty. I felt I had let myself down before I even started.

Obviously, this is not a mindset which helped set me up for success. I needed a new approach. I needed a way to get that "fresh start" without having to wait for the following morning.

I remembered from my research about quitting that cigarette withdrawal symptoms (though they called them "cravings," grrr....) usually last between 3 to 7 minutes.

This brightened my mood considerably! I might not have been able to make it a whole day right out of the gate, but I know I could make it through 3 minutes. I felt that with some practice, I could make it through 7 minutes. *That's when I realized that if I could make it through ten minutes, I could make it through anything.*

They tell you to do things during your withdrawal symptoms like drink water, or distract yourself with something. I absolutely agree, especially with water. Drinking water was one of the most important things to me, and I could tell it was helping wash out the nicotine and other countless chemicals from my system.

The problem was, drinking water and spinning around looking for distractions soon became a combination of frustrating and boring. There are only so many times a person can gulp 16 ounces of water and walk back and forth from the mailbox. Finding a distraction, any distraction, made me just that: A distracted person! Who has time to be a distracted person?

There was also an added complication becoming more and more clear to me. Drinking water is good, yes. Finding random things to distract myself from nicotine desire is good, yes. But I found myself at a loss when I realized that when the withdrawals finally subsided, and when I was over the toughest part of quitting, I would still be a lost-feeling, distracted person whose identity had been ransacked by nicotine.

I needed a plan. I needed a strategy.

That's when I decided to use the waves of withdrawal to my advantage. I decided to make them work *for* me, instead of having to simply endure them until they magically stopped happening. I decided to make a list of activities and keep them at-the-ready. However, these activities would be special because they would focus on behaviors that would help me nourish and encourage my positive sense of self....aka Healing the whole reason I had gotten stuck addicted to nicotine in the first place!

Some of these activities could have been rushed to fit three minutes. Others could have been stretched into bigger projects that lasted all day. I decided ten minutes was the perfect time. This way, I could be sure to pass that three-minute mark. Ten minutes was also enough time for my mind to feel really invested in the activity I was doing. I saw that ten minutes was enough for me to really begin to teach myself new habits and behaviors, not just distract myself from the old ones. It was enough time to really start to experience the feelings of being a non-smoker. I was confident that after a while, I would *be* a non-smoker. More than this: I would be a fully-formed, well-rounded person with real life experience in healthy behaviors because of all the time I had spent working on them!

I couldn't do a whole day at first. But I could certainly do ten minutes.

This strategy worked for me better than my wildest dreams! I was no longer afraid of withdrawal symptoms because I knew how to use them proactively, for the benefit of my body and my soul. I had developed a system that really, truly gave me experience living the life of my dreams. During what I expected would be one of the most difficult periods of my life so far, I actually begun enjoying my life more than I ever had! It was also at this point that I simply knew in my heart: This was the quit that was going to last.

I am going to give you all my strategies and behaviors for you to try out yourself! If you're ready to let go of the fear, and ready to start your new life as a non-smoker, I hope you'll find some great ideas in this book. Even more than that, I hope you'll add behaviors and affirmations of your own to practice, and to restore and rebuild the wonderful, beautiful soul that is Y-O-U.

A Couple Tips Before You Start

If you're anything like me, then trust me; once we get going on our behavioral strategy for quitting, you'll start to feel some anticipatory excitement about the whole thing. You might even go so far as to genuinely start to look forward to doing it! I know, I know: Unbelievable, right? But it's true!

Since I know the momentum is so helpful, I don't want to interrupt things for you once you get going by pummeling you with a whole bunch more information. That's why I've spent so much time in this book so far giving you background information to consider while you pump yourself up in preparation for your quit.

I just want to take a tiny chapter to give you a few more tips before things really get cooking. I wish I had known these things before. I feel that it would have made the whole process a lot easier.

Some Tips Before You Quit:

Tip #1

It is very possible that your appetite is going to increase. Mine did, at least. It felt like I was genuinely hungry for the first time in years. Hey, with cigarettes suppressing my appetite so effectively, it probably *was* the first time I was genuinely hungry in years! I'm talking about the raw, all-consuming hunger that can turn even the most disciplined person into a ravenous beast, capable of decimating whole pizzas in a single sitting. For me, it made sense to think of the quitting experience as something that involves all of my instincts, at every level. I reminded myself that the reaction is one that is concerned for my very survival (an illusion that felt incredibly real to my body). It's a lot easier to feel peaceful about survival with a full tummy.

My point is that it is likely very possible that you will have those same moments of ravenous hunger. Plan accordingly. Anticipate that you will likely reach with gusto for whatever is closest to you. Make sure that whatever is closest to you is NOT PIZZA, for goodness' sakes. Consider keeping yourself well-stocked in raw vegetables which will provide you with vitamins, minerals, a satisfying crunch for your mouth, and will promote healing without adding excess calories. Fresh, raw veggies are also a great source of fiber, which can help you with:

Tip #2

Let's just get this out there....cigarettes help you poop. They might not help everybody, but the vast majority of cigarette smokers I have spoken to really appreciate the boost in firepower, shall we say. That being said, guess what happens when the nicotine is no longer in your system? That's right: The gas tank is empty. Actually, strike that: The tank quickly becomes very, very FULL, especially as your appetite increases. I think it takes a little while for the body to get accustomed again to doing things on its own. When I quit, I really wished I had started increasing my fiber or utilizing a stool softener a few days, or even a week, *before* my quit date. There, I said it. (Now we know each other better than either of us bargained for.)

Tip #3

This is probably still my favorite discovery. This tip energized me, invigorated me, lifted my mood, and gave me a much-needed mental reset on all counts, as a matter of fact. I'm talking about a good, old-fashioned nap! Ten (or fifteen) minutes of quiet, comfortable sleep time was all it took for me to gain huge benefits. Nicotine is a stimulant, so after it was no longer in my system, I found myself feeling quite weak very often. I was also more inclined to be irritable with those around me, and to feel pretty pouty about my situation in general. Taking little catnaps helped me recover on physical levels, as well as on emotional levels.

"I haven't taken a nap since I was a baby," you might say. Yes, babies and little kids need naps. Their little systems are building themselves from the ground up. They literally simply aren't big enough to sustain activity all day without rest. Guess what: When you quit smoking cigarettes, the operations of your body must build themselves from the ground up all over again. I didn't just enjoy naps. I needed them.

I didn't let myself get excessive about it. I think it's good to be conscious of the quality of your rest, without obsessing over it. Ten minutes is certainly good enough. Trust me: You used to spend ten minutes on a cigarette break, several times a day. You have time to take a teeny nap instead, and your entire world will thank you for it.

Tip #4

After a couple of weeks into my quit, I started coughing, which produced some gross results. My doctor told me that this was some tar, which had been trapped inside my lungs, and now my body was finally able to start getting rid of it. Gross, right? News flash: YOU'RE not gross. But cigarettes? Yeah, they are definitely gross. Anyway, my doctor also told me that there would likely be more tar to come, though it would be less and less over time. I know this is probably so much more information than you bargained for, but I'm letting you know of this element so you won't panic if it happens to you. I also want to remind you not to go through any of this alone. Any funny business happens during your quit, call your doctor.

I also saw this as an opportunity to congratulate myself. I felt that even though the process was awkward, I felt validated by my cough. I felt I was getting rid of toxicity in my life, both literally and figuratively. I hope you give yourself a pat on the back for this, too.

Tip #5

Find a Quit Counselor. Research free programs. Search the internet for as much free information as you can find. Read about quitting smoking like it's a part-time job. Get informed. Research the different ways people quit smoking. If you're thinking about quitting, *keep thinking about it.* Find forums overseen by qualified professionals. Get your doctor involved. **I absolutely did NOT endeavor to quit smoking alone.** It made all the difference to me to have someone holding me accountable and giving me reliable, medical, evidence-based information in order to keep myself healthy. Had I relapsed, I would have already had someone to go to for help to get back on track. I highly recommend anyone who wants to address nicotine addiction to *seek qualified allies.* Yes, you are the only person responsible for your success, but that does not mean that you have to do this all by yourself. Be wise. Seek help.

Tip #6

Select a quit date. I almost didn't mention this tip because I found it in almost every piece of smoking cessation literature I could find. I don't want to take it for granted, though: It's good advice. Have a quit date. Put it on the calendar. Tell your family about it. And get your plan together.

Tip #7

I was awfully scared of missing that first cigarette of the day. I was the type to have one with a cup of coffee, five or ten minutes after getting up in the morning. What really helped me was actually having a plan for what I would do in the morning instead of smoking that first cigarette. I tried a few different things, but my favorite was bringing a piece of buttered toast with me to accompany my morning cup of coffee. I chose high quality butter and bread that had lots of nuts and seeds in it. The crunch of the toast was comforting. Something about the fat content in the butter and the nuts was really comforting to my system. This toast trick really helped me minimize my anxiety, and soon enough I was sailing through my wake-up time looking forward to toast, and not missing that morning cigarette at all.

The Drinking Straw Technique

...aka My solution to address quit anxiety, the need for hydration, and calm my oral fixation symptoms.

This is a simple technique I developed while quitting. Supplies needed are simply a glass of water and a drinking straw. This technique is my final tip, and probably the one that helped me the most. If you take anything from this chapter with you on your own quit journey, I hope this is something that helps you along too.

First, I found it very comforting to my nerves to practice breathing. I learned some yogic breathing from a local yoga studio, but most of the time I didn't use any over-complicated breathing techniques. Cigarette smokers, I have learned, learn to breathe very shallowly. I knew any kind of breathing would work wonders for replenishing the oxygen levels of my system, and re-teaching my diaphragm to breathe well, deeply, and happily.

The breathing I used for the Drinking Straw Technique was first a deep inhale through my nose. I felt my stomach expand from air, and then my chest. Then I would release the air, feeling my torso deflate in reverse: Chest went down, then stomach. I released the air through my mouth, making an "O" shape with my lips. It was exactly the same mouth shape I used to expel smoke from my cigarettes. This solved half of the so-called "oral fixation" people find so difficult to overcome.

After a deep breath, I would take a sip of that cool, clean water through my straw. I made the same shape with my lips over the straw as I used to when inhaling the smoke from my cigarettes.

It's as simple as that! Breathing in through my nose, then blowing the air out through my mouth. Then, a sip of water. All the motions of smoking, but in a slightly different order and purpose, in order to keep myself hydrated and detoxing. Nerves calmed, check. More oxygen in my system, check. Hydrated for health and detox, check.

I never did this to the point of being light-headed, but if that had happened, I would have *stopped doing it.* So if you get light-headed, you know. Stop it.

Make It A Game

Aka: "I can have *fun* while recovering from nicotine addiction?!" (The answer is: YES!)

Here's a recap: My life was changed forever when I quit smoking. This was not just because I detoxified my life of harmful habits, but also because I *used the recovery process to my advantage* by taking opportunities to practice new habits. These habits supported healing my own sense of self worth, and paved the way for personal freedom. The best part: I could make huge progress by approaching these new habits **ten minutes at a time.**

That's why this is **The Ten Minute Quit**, folks!

Think about this for a moment: With the health risks, the huge levels of guilt to bear every single day as a cigarette smoker, the pressure from society, the pressure from our family and friends, the times we needed to catch our breath, not to mention the nicotine invader that has ransacked our personalities and stolen our abilities to count ourselves as truly free souls....with all this going on, HAVEN'T WE SUFFERED ENOUGH?!

Beating yourself up about smoking cigarettes hasn't worked. That's why you're reading this book! The guilt trips and scare tactics don't work. That's why you've still been smoking cigarettes! It's time to stop the suffering.

Forget paying our dues. We've paid them. You can interpret that literally or figuratively, and it would still be true. We've paid for carton after carton of cigarettes. This money could have gone to so many other things. Yes, this was a choice, and the result of our weakened willpower, but it wasn't a good choice, and so we have suffered. Don't we teach children that they must make good choices, or else they will endure difficult consequences? Why should we think the rules change just because we've gotten old enough to legally buy tobacco products? For anyone who is not a cigarette smoker: Do you have any idea how damaging it is to feel guilty about smoking cigarettes, but lack the tools to break free of it? It's a prison. It can very quickly become a personal hell, because it erodes our sense of self worth when we choose time and time again to do the thing we know is hurting us--but we feel we "have" to when our biological systems have been tricked into literally saying that we need this substance in order to survive.

No more suffering. No more guilt. We're not going to approach this from a mindset of shame.

My goal is to be a good friend to you during this process. As your friend, I think it's important to tell you what society likely won't.

You have already suffered enough. You are not worthless. You are not ruined. It's not over. You've had years of this garbage in your system, and that's long enough. It will simply not do to dread some sort of oncoming crucible as you change your life. You've been chained to nicotine for who knows how long. You've been imprisoned already. You've already done your time; you've already completed your sentence. The world may have consequences, and the world is entitled to have consequences. We all have to get along with the world. But, you don't have to wait for the world to give you permission to let go of feeling ashamed. You can let that shame go.

You can start today, by taking a lighter, loving

approach to yourself to get this job done. No excuses, no self pity. Only forgiveness, and determination.

This is my main inspiration for the approach I took to learning new behaviors about the kind of person I knew myself to be, and the kind of person I wanted to be. I didn't put myself through a "regimen."

I made it a game.

Make It A Game!

This is not exactly a new idea. Look around, and you'll see nannies putting spoonfuls of sugar in medicine and apps that help you create a superhero version of yourself to emulate and ultimately become. Look everywhere, and you can find tools galore specifically for quitting smoking, which help us "play" on our smartphones while we quit. There are even decades of recordings from hypnotists, giving us positive, non-smoking messages so that we can quit while we're leisurely enjoying something else. I say, if any of these tools help you feel empowered, great!

But chances are, you'll be back to buy another one. And another one. Hey, money spent on your education in smoking cessation is better than money spent on your addiction, so go for it! I spent a few dollars on some of these myself.

My offerent to this swirling sea of choices is a game I designed for myself, by myself. I made it quickly, and I made it for cheap. Seriously, it was dirt cheap. The way this system was different than all the others was that it didn't simply distract me while my body adjusted to quitting. This made it so that I was quitting, *and liked it.* Crazy, right?

Here are the supplies I used:

Index cards from the dollar store
Glass marbles from the dollar store
2 large votive holders from the dollar store
...that's about it.

I filled one votive holder with the glass marbles, and left the other one empty.

On every index card, I wrote the behavior or affirmation I wanted in my life. I didn't write the cards like instructions. I wrote them in a very special way, which I'll get to in the next section.

Every time I had a wave of withdrawal symptoms, I drew a card and practiced the behavior or affirmation I had written on it. Every time I completed a card, I put it in a pile to the side. I also moved one glass marble from one votive holder to another. When the holder was full, I gave myself a treat!

All In The Cards

This is a huge point, and a huge secret to my success. I've already told you that every one of my cards contained a behavior which I could practice during my waves of withdrawal symptoms. I took things a step further in the *way* I wrote the cards. I put each behavior into the format of a statement about myself. Here's an example:

I know that making the bed in the morning is a healthy, civilized habit that has some psychological benefits. If making the bed was something I was going to practice, I wouldn't worry about what time of day it was.

Whenever that ol' wave of withdrawal symptoms came around, that's when I'd be practicing this particular behavior. If the bed was made already, I would go smooth out the sheets. Or, I would take a ten minute nap, and then whoops: look who gets to make the bed again, just like on my card! It's repetitive, I know. But, it's a behavior that I would get to practice, and it certainly beats smoking cigarettes or walking to the mailbox for the thousandth time!

If I were to put "making the bed" on an index card so that I would have a task ready-to-go for withdrawal time, I would use the opportunity to write a statement that healed and affirmed my identity. I would write:

"I am a person who makes the bed."

This went exactly the same way for *every single behavior*. My "I am a person who..." statements ranged to include everything from "I am a person who is caught up with my ironing," to "I am a person who is getting her college degree," to "I am a person who walks the dog."

I felt such a sense of righteous defiance when I wrote those cards for the first time. I had exposed my nicotine addiction for what it was: a huge leech that had taken over my reflection, my self-awareness, and my identity. At this point, I knew nicotine could never agian tell me who I am. I'm the one who told me who I am. I would be 100% responsible for my own life and happiness, an dl would become the best there has ever been at being me, ten minutes, and one behavior card at a time.

I am a person who practices forgiveness.
I am a person who reads cookbooks.
I am a person who was created by God.
I am a person who wakes up early in the mornings.
I am a person.
I am a person.
I am a human person.

I am a human person who is loved, and who is loving. Who makes mistakes. Who started smoking cigarettes. Who stopped smoking cigarettes. Who learns new things every day. Who is one among billions with her own problems and battles to face. Who becomes kinder and more compassionate to those around her by better understanding herself.

I am a human person. And so are you.

So what if it takes the rest of the world a little while to catch on to who you are. Don't wait for them. Go BE who you are! If you don't know how, then I am personally inviting you to find out, and to do so in a fun, effective, and truly rewarding way!

Speaking of Rewards

I believe in taking time to celebrate accomplishments. I think it's great if you are able to reward yourself with things that are meaningful and enjoyable to you. This might mean hiring a babysitter and having a date night with your spouse. It could also mean that you finally get to try that new burger place in town. Go buy that pair of earrings you've been eyeing. Go do that hike you felt guilty or insecure about because you were afraid you'd get out of breath.

Whatever you do, however, do NOT reward yourself with cigarettes. I feel that this should go without saying, but you have to remember that cigarette smoking is something that you USED to do. If you smoke a cigarette, you'll have to start all those waves of withdrawal symptoms all over again, and it's just not worth it.

Don't smoke cigarettes. Do fun stuff instead!

Write some things you can do to reward yourself whenever your marble jar is full:

_____

_____

_____

_____

_____

_____

_____

_____

_____

When You're on the Clock

Unless we happen to have been born in just the right conditions, chances are that sooner or later, we'll all have to go to work. Managing waves of withdrawal symptoms while on the job uses the same approach as the behaviors you can practice in your personal life. If you are employed, try to find a blank copy of the form used for performance reviews. If that's not accessible, see if you can find a job description of the position you currently have, *and* the position that you perhaps would *like* to have. Study which behaviors and characteristics are valuable to the industry you're working in. Put them on index cards, and put them into practice! By the time you view yourself as a non-smoker, you'll also be a highly qualified professional in your industry, who is also highly deserving of a promotion, if you ask me.

If you're self-employed, the success of your business is actually what gives you the review on how well (or not) you are performing in your industry. Why not study the greatest or most innovative thinkers in the business you're a part of? Somewhere along the line, you'll likely uncover actions these people took, or philosophies they had, which you can translate to behaviors for your index cards.

Are you starting to see how we can really use our withdrawal symptoms to our advantage? Most approaches to quitting simply help us "deal" with these withdrawals. This book outlines how to use them as a driving force of good in our lives. Neat, right?

Failure Days

We all have days when it seems like nothing goes right. There were definitely days when I felt positively pouty, and nothing could convince me to get up, drink water, or do anything but moan for at least an hour. On these days, I would get to one card, maybe two. I would have some form of junk food. If this ever happens to you, my advice is not to beat yourself up about it. Recovering from nicotine is hard work, and it is something to work on over time. If you totally fail practicing your new way of doing things, my advice is to just relax. You're not going to excuse yourself from getting the job done (right?), so take a rest for an hour or two, and then get back to it.

See these times as a *good thing*. Why? Because by setting your cards down and coming back to them in a couple hours, you are teaching yourself that you are trustworthy when it comes to not giving up. You are teaching yourself that you can get frustrated, and still not smoke. Every time you return to your cards, you are teaching yourself that you can feel fed-up and stressed out, and that you can still trust yourself to make good decisions.

Think about it: This is great practice for life! How wonderful it will be when you can face the stressful parts of your life, and know beyond the shadow of a doubt that no matter how you may feel, you simply are not going to be smoking cigarettes again. You can finally trust yourself. How wonderful to have experiences and memories of yourself doing exactly this, and being reliable and successful at it.

See? Failure days are not really failures at all. It's all good!

Level 1: Acceptance

It's finally time to start our game! You made it! My advice to you is to start this level *before* your quit date. This way, you'll have tons of positive and productive self-talk happening during the first part of your transition to a non smoker.

I have written these levels as they appeared in my journal, and in my notes as I played the game for myself. Feel free to change the wording so it fits YOU and YOUR goals!

Ready? Here we go!

Level Goals:
Facing the truth about cigarette smoking, facing the truth about the human condition, facing the truth about what I really, truly want for myself and my life.

My Goals:

(What I know I must Accept About Quitting Smoking:)

_____

_____

MY LEVEL 1 INDEX CARD STATEMENTS:

(Reminder: Write ONE statement per card!)

I accept that it is time for me to quit smoking cigarettes.

I accept that I am not an exception when it comes to the health risks associated with smoking cigarettes.

I accept that smoking puts my health in danger.

I accept the fact that I am learning how to make better choices.

I accept the fact that I am learning better coping skills.

I accept the fact that there is a new way of living which I have never tried before now.

I accept that this is a process.

I accept that this will take time.

I accept ALL responsibility for my happiness.

I accept ALL responsibility and consequences of my choices.

I accept FULL responsibility for my recovery.

I accept that parts of this process will be easy for me.

I accept that parts of this process will be difficult for me.

I accept that there are times when I will need to ask for help.

I accept that people around me may not understand what I am going through.

I accept that people around me may change their opinions about me in some way after I quit.

I accept that the people around me may say/do judgemental things about me or my quit process, and that these things are NONE of my business.

I accept that it is my responsibility to manage when I am tired.

I accept that it is my responsibility to manage when I am cranky.

I accept that it is my responsibility to manage when I am lonely.

I accept that it is my responsibility to manage when I am hungry.

I accept the role of a loving parent over myself during my recovery.

I accept the fact that I am worthy of love.

I accept the fact that I must let go of the past.

I accept the fact that I must find a way to forgive people who have hurt me, even if they are never ever going to apologize.

I accept the fact that I must learn to forgive myself.

I accept the fact that I must treat people with dignity and respect, even and especially during my recovery.

I accept that mismanaged anger will make this process even longer.

I accept all the rewards of quitting smoking cigarettes.

I accept all improvements to my health after quitting smoking.

I accept feeling proud of myself for the hard work I am doing mentally, physically, emotionally, and spiritually.

I accept this feeling of accomplishment about how far I have come.

I accept all my positive feelings about the future.

I accept feeling happy.

I accept feeling grateful.

I accept--without judgement--any and every truth I discover about myself.

Be sure to make an index card for each one of your goals regarding what you know you must accept about yourself and your situation. Keep them positive and truthful. No negativity is allowed here...for example, "I accept that my husband/wife/mother/father is the reason I started smoking because he is an unsupportive, lazy bum" is just being childish, and shifting blame and responsibility off of yourself. I don't know your husband/wife/great-uncle, and it doesn't really matter to your goal of saving your identity from nicotine. This is *your* quit, *your* health, and *your* responsibility. You can assess any life changes after you are free from nicotine. Your quit is the priority at this point in your life, and you'll get farther by being positive and holding *yourself* accountable *first*.

Remember:

This level is all about rewarding our brains for truthful, productive, and positive thinking. Therefore, simply reminding yourself about these, using them as affirmations, and really taking a moment to just let them sink in, totally merits putting a marble in your jar (or whatever you're using to store them in)!

You may feel that this is somehow "cheating" since obviously this level can get the marbles moving pretty quickly. You are absolutely *not* cheating, however. Managing your nicotine detox is a great big deal, and we all deserve as much encouragement and positivity as we can possibly get. Society is not so great at dishing this out, but you know what? That shouldn't matter. We can give ourselves the love. We can give ourselves the encouragement. We can give ourselves the boost we need to face the bright light of truth and to **get the job done**.

We can do this! You can do this!

On Feeling Guilt or Shame:
If you're feeling guilty about rewarding yourself so quickly in this way, I think maybe your levels of personal shame are likely a bit out of balance. I don't believe anyone should feel ashamed about working towards their health. You are a mortal human being, and that means you can only make choices forwards, not backward. We are ALL subject to this rule. It's part of the human condition.

Therefore, it is not for anyone else to say whether or not you deserve your health.

Don't forget about your rewards system too! When you fill up a container with marbles, you should go to your plan for rewards, and totally take yourself up on one of them. You deserve it! Your brain deserves it too. After all, isn't positive reinforcement a method we might use to teach children about desired patterns and behaviors? Who is to say we haven't outgrown that approach for ourselves? Give your brain a treat, and do this level once, twice, or as many times as you feel you need to before your quit date in order to start changing your thinking patterns. Do these cards right when you get up in the morning. Do the cards even if you are reading them during your morning cigarette. If it makes those morning cigarettes less appealing, guess what: you're seeing the truth about them more and more each day.

When you're ready, set your quit date.

Keep on thinking about those good, truthful things as your quit date approaches. Keep it up, keep going, don't back down, and don't stop.

Get going on increasing that fiber intake too (seriously)...you'll thank me for this later!

The night before your quit date, prepare the next level of index cards. Have them ready to go for you to use. These will be behaviors you can practice after your bare minimum coping skills (drinking water, distracting yourself, the Drinking Straw Technique, etc.).

Congratulations on making it through Level 1!

Now it is time to quit smoking!

Keep practicing your acceptance affirmations until your quit date arrives!

When your quit date arrives, it'll be time to start incorporating Level 2.

Level 2: Achieving Authentic Rest

Why "authentic" rest? I use this word just to show that this is a time to heal the system from being constantly pummelled by the stimulant of nicotine. I think when we are chock-full of stimulation, chemical or otherwise, we don't really rest. We crash. Then it's up-and-at-it-again, until our next crash time.

No more of that, please and thank you. It's time to finally get to stop running this horrible addiction-laden race. It's time to get to join the human race, where people actually sleep during the night, and electricity is still fairly new in our human heritage. It's time to get to relax when the sun goes down instead of artificially pushing ourselves beyond biology. It's time to contemplate daytime and nighttime. It's time to understand that there is a time to work, or for activities, or to press onward, and then there is also a time to relax, to recharge, and to have peace.

With that in mind, here are the things I put on my index cards to help uncover the parts of me which are full of peacefulness and restorative quiet.

Level Goals:

Managing my system "reboot" to get enough rest during the first part of my nicotine withdrawals, building appropriate sleep habits, supporting my taxed nervous system, generating feelings of peace.

My Goals:

(What I know about the Rest I Need Right Now:)

_____

_____

MY LEVEL 2 INDEX CARD STATEMENTS:

(Reminder: Write ONE statement per card!)

Let's pretend a withdrawal is going to hit right now. In this moment, you'll say to yourself "I'm not a person who smokes cigarettes…."

"I am a person with a bedtime."

- Figure out how much sleep you ought to be getting. From there, decide what time of night will give you that amount of sleep! Guess what: this is your bedtime. Protect your bedtime. Love your bedtime. Soon, you'll get to look forward to, enjoy, and be grateful for this wonderful time of day. If you find yourself needing more sleep, change to an earlier time. If you find yourself needing less sleep, change to a later time. Simple!

- If you pull this card during a time of day when it is not yet time to go to sleep, you can still reaffirm this behavior by taking a moment *right now* to set a "bedtime" reminder on your smartphone. This little alarm will let you know when it's time for you to start getting ready. You can also do little things that will prepare you for your day tomorrow so that when it does come time to catch those zzz's, you'll be able to relax, knowing you're prepared for the following day.

- Ten Minute Bedtime Prep ideas: THIS IS WHAT YOU DO DURING WITHDRAWALS, WHEN YOU DRAW THIS CARD! Take ten minutes to set a bedtime alarm, fluff your pillows, pack your lunch for tomorrow, launder and press your outfit for the next day, set the coffeemaker to automatic timer, make a To-Do list for tomorrow so you don't have to think about it later, finish tougher tasks today so that you don't have to worry about them tonight, shop for comfy pajamas online, etc.

My Ten Minute Bedtime Ideas:

_____

_____

"I am a person with a Rise Time"

- Just like having a bedtime will help you ensure that you are consistently getting enough sleep, having a rise time will help further encourage and support this health on the other side of your sleep schedule.
- Same idea as bedtime: If you pull this card during a withdrawal sometime in the day, why not take a moment to make sure you have an alarm set for the time you need to get up? What are some rituals which might help you have a brighter, happier rise in the morning?
- Ten Minute Rise Time Prep Ideas: Wash, fold, and put away laundry, clean up your bedroom, plan a delicious breakfast for tomorrow, create a morning

ritual, spend ten minutes researching the morning rituals of successful people, etc.

My Ten Minute Rise Time Ideas:

_____

_____

"I am a person who studies breathing techniques."

Spend ten minutes doing one of these things:

- Study about breathing techniques online.
- Practice a breathing technique you have learned.
- Practice your new favorite breathing technique.
- Smell fruit and coffee at the grocery store.
- Go smell anything! Notice how your sense of smell is improving day by day.
- Go outside, doing nothing but breathing the free air without being pumped full of smoke. Breathe in that freedom. You've earned it.

My Ideas for Ten-Minute Breath Breaks:

_____

_____

"I am a person who is learning how to meditate."

Spend ten minutes at a time on some of these things instead of smoking:

- Research how to meditate.
- Shop for a book about meditation.
- Learn how meditation is done in different cultures and religions.
- Read about meditation.
- Try to meditate for a few minutes.
- Find an expert on meditation and look at their social media.
- Try meditating again.
- Keep trying meditation. Notice how you approach it and how it feels to practice this over time.

My Ideas for Ten-Minute Meditations:

_____

_____

"I am a person who creates a restful environment."

Spend ten minutes on some of these:

- Straighten things up around whatever area you're in. Your mama was right: a messy bed makes a messy head.

- Clear anything work-related out of your bedroom. The bedroom is not for work.
- Create relaxed lighting.
- Buy or search online for battery-operated string lights or LED candles.
- Dust your bedroom and really put some elbow grease in it.
- Change as much furniture around as you can in ten minutes.
- Buy a houseplant.
- Care for your houseplant.
- Wash your bedroom window, both sides, if possible. Let all that good light in.
- Play soothing music.
- Enjoy a ten-minute nap!

My Ideas for Ten-Minute Downtime:

_____

_____

...are you starting to get the idea that each card has actions you can take to fill a ten-minute timeframe and prompt you to practice being the person you'd like to be?

"I am a person who makes the bed."

Spend ten minutes on some of these:

- Make the bed, if it isn't made already.
- Watch a video online about housekeeping.
- Learn how to do hospital corners on bed sheets.
- Crochet a blanket to improve your bed.
- Smooth out all the sheets. Pretend you're ironing the sheets with your hands.
- Make sure your pajamas are cared for and put away.
- Take ten minutes to iron your pajamas. Give yourself the royal treatment!

My Ideas for Ten-Minute Bed Makeover:

_____

_____

"I am a person who writes in a journal."

Spend ten minutes on some of these:

- Write what you're grateful for.
- Vent about anything and everything that is stressing you out today.
- Just write about how your life is going.
- Write about a happy childhood memory.

My Ideas for Ten-Minute Reflections:

_____

_____

"I am a person who drinks hot tea."

Spend ten minutes on some of these:

- Sip tea ever so slowly for ten minutes.
- Research tea ceremonies around the world.
- Engage all your senses by brewing an attractive-looking strength, enjoy the scent, feel the hot cup, listen to music or enjoy silence, taste your tea slowly.

My Ideas for a Ten-Minute Teatime:

_____

_____

What are some habits you can develop to help yourself have a bedtime at the same time each day? What things really get on your nerves during the day, and how can you change your mindset or circumstances to address and cope with them? What helps you feel grateful? What helps you feel peaceful? Turn all of these things into more cards, and plan several actions you can take to promote these things in your life. This way, when those withdrawals hit, you can *transform* that time into actions that equate to more peace, more rest, and more restoration in your life.

Congratulations!

Congratulations on completing Level 2! I hope you'll keep adding more cards as you continue to have ideas about what authentic rest means for you and your life.

Can you describe who you want to be in regards to rest? Take some time to think about your relationship with rest, and how you can use your recovery time to transform this relationship for the better.

Write your statements here for future cards:

I am a person who:_____.

I am a person who:_____.

I am a person who:_____.

I am a person who:_____.

I am a person who:_____.

I am a person who:_____.

I am a person who:_____.

I am a person who:_____.

I am a person who:_____.

I am a person who:_____.

I am a person who:_____.

I am a person who:_____.

Where Do My Used Cards Go?

Just a reminder: You should keep cycling through all of your cards all the time! Now that you've introduced Level 2 into your life, you should keep practicing these things by combining them with your Level 1 cards. Keep cycling through them until you are comfortable enough to move forward with the next level of your quit! Don't forget to reward yourself!

My Card Pile

Here are all the cards you should have in your card pile:

Level 1: Acceptance
Level 2: Achieving Authentic Rest

Keep cycling through them!

Don't forget to move a marble from one glass container to the other for every card you practice during your withdrawal symptoms.

When your glass container is full of marbles, use your rewards system plan to reward yourself!

Level 3: Physical

I know, I know: As if the body wasn't already doing a ton of stuff at this point, now we are adding physical health to our recovery. Just as a reminder of how things should be progressing: If you are working through your cards the same way I did, by now you'll have added Level 3 cards to a growing pile *also containing Levels 1 and 2.* Even though it is probably very likely that you are feeling fatigued from the lack of stimulant coursing through your veins, fear not. Though this level focuses more on physical activity, continuing the other levels as well means you'll also get chances to rest and replenish your motivation.

Level Goals:

Using physical activity to manage stress and promote healing, cardiovascular considerations, good diet and nutrition habits, vitamins and supplements .

My Goals:

(What I know I must Address About My Physical Health:)

_____

_____

MY LEVEL 3 INDEX CARD STATEMENTS:

(Reminder: Write ONE statement per card!)

"I am a person who does excercise for fun."

Spend ten minutes at a time practicing one of these behaviors:

- Even if I have never viewed myself in this way before, I know that it's inside me. What exercise do I really enjoy? Sweeping the floor? Doing sit-ups?
- Do an internet search of exercises that can be done at the dest, on the couch, outside, inside while staying in bed, while a person is recovering, etc.
- Make cards for each of the exercises you find to prompt yourself to practice them throughout the day!
- Do an exercise you already know that you love.
- Dance around like a crazy person for ten minutes.

My Ideas to Get Myself Moving for Ten Minutes:

_____

_____

"I am a person who stays busy."

Spend ten minutes at a time practicing one of these behaviors:

- Your lazy days are over. Cover the couch with something so you won't be tempted to sit on your patootie all day.
- No moping around allowed. Mopping instead! Clean those floors!
- Housework is an incredible workout.
- Clean those walls!
- Clean the inside of the kitchen cabinets.
- Clean out your desk.
- Clean a junk drawer.
- Clean your workspace.

My Ideas, aka If There's Time to Lean, There's Time to Clean:

_____

_____

"I am a person who eats breakfast."

Spend ten minutes at a time practicing one of these behaviors:

- Do an internet search about healthy recovery breakfasts. We are recovering patients, after all!
- Shop for the breakfast items you'll need this week.
- Prepare the ingredients for your breakfast tomorrow.
- Sit at the table if it's breakfast time, and slowly enjoy each bite.
- Make more cards for lunch and dinner!

My Ideas for Restorative Meal Times:

_____

_____

"I am a person who has a healthy relationship with food."

Spend ten minutes at a time practicing one of these behaviors:

- Search on the internet for information about healthy relationships to food.
- Shop for a book about nutrition.
- Read about proper nutrition.

- Visualize what a healthy meal might be for each time of day. Include snacks. Write your thoughts in your journal.
- Clear your table, or tidy up wherever you plan to sit and eat your meals. Designate this space for nourishment times only.

My Ideas for My Relationship with Food:

_____

_____

"I am a person who cares for my muscles."
Spend ten minutes at a time practicing one of these behaviors:

- Give yourself a foot massage.
- Massage your hands.
- Stretch your legs.
- Stretch your arms and roll your shoulders.

My Ideas for Ten-Minute Muscle Care:

_____

_____

"I am a person who manages my health."

Spend ten minutes at a time practicing one of these behaviors:

- Research which doctors you could see for a check-up.
- Write down anything you may have ever wanted to ask a doctor.
- Write down anything you have been too shy to ask a doctor.
- Research which dentists you could see for a cleaning.
- Look at what your options are for getting a vision or hearing check-up.

My Ideas for Ten Minute Health Tune-Ups:

_____

_____

"I am a person with impeccable grooming."

Spend ten minutes at a time practicing one of these behaviors:

- Wash your face gently and lovingly with mild soap.
- Use a facial toner for the skin on your face and neck.
- Do your makeup and/or groom your facial hair.

- Moisturize your face.
- Get out that mud mask!
- Tweeze your eyebrows.
- Try a new lipstick.

My Ideas for Ten-Minute Spa Breaks:

_____

_____

These were some of my ideas for the kind of person I wanted to be in regards to my physical health! I shared them in the hopes that they could get you started. Take some time to think about the kind of person you want to be in regards to your physical health. Can you describe yourself when it comes to your health?

Write your statements here for future cards:

I am a person who:_____.

I am a person who:_____.

I am a person who:_____.

I am a person who:_____.

I am a person who:_____.

I am a person who:_____.

I am a person who:_____.

I am a person who:_____.

I am a person who:_____.

I am a person who:_____.

I am a person who:_____.

I am a person who:_____.

Congratulations!

Congratulations on successfully integrating Level 3 cards into your life! Each step you take leads you further and further toward the life of your dreams, and your life as a non-smoker! Keep it up!

My Card Pile

Here are all the cards you should have in your card pile:

Level 1: Acceptance

Level 2: Achieving Authentic Rest

Level 3: Physical

Keep cycling through them!

Don't forget to move a marble from one glass container to the other for every card you practice during your withdrawal symptoms.

When your glass container is full of marbles, use your rewards system plan to reward yourself!

Level 4: Mental

I really feel that we are currently enjoying a period in society which has an unprecedented amount of awareness and appreciation for mental health. There is so much information out there. It makes me think that the mental health professionals around must be really achieving new levels of understanding and training. It's an exciting time to address mental health!

Just like our physical and emotional health, I view mental health as my personal responsibility, first and foremost. I don't need a doctor to tell me to brush my teeth every day, for example. I can brush my teeth at appropriate times without medical advice, and this certainly goes a long way towards keeping me happy and healthy (not to mention, other people enjoy being around me a little more when my teeth are brushed). Just like this example, I believe there are great habits we can build to support our mental health, and these can be done every day to keep our minds happy and healthy.

When I addressed these habits myself, I realized that the temptation for me was to really try on my own to get to the root cause of why I started smoking in the first place. This was a lot of emotional and psychological work. To be honest, I still don't know "The" answer. I suspect the underlying reason for my smoking cigarettes in the first place has several factors in it combined with time, and not just one single reason. If I felt I needed to understand all these factors in order to have peace about these things, you can bet your bottom dollar that I would be in the waiting room of a qualified therapist ASAP. For anyone who simply cannot let these things go, I just want you to know: You aren't alone, and it's ok to need help. Get help. You don't have to do this alone. Don't be alone in this.

I really do believe that we all struggle with many different factors, not just one. Because we are real, valuable, human persons, we deserve to have some help to heal when we need it.

If you find yourself grappling with the underlying issues of some of the more painful things in your life experience, please don't despair. Do what you can in the moment and seek help for whatever is too big for you to handle during your recovery time. My self-reflection always included asking "Do I have enough peace about this to stop having to think about it all the time?" If I did, I went on with my life. If I couldn't stop thinking about it, I knew I wasn't over it, and I knew I could figure out why somehow--either on my own, or with the help of a trained mental health professional.

Here are some of the habits I practiced when I took charge of becoming my own advocate for mental health!

Level Goals:
Psychological health, forgiveness of self and others, self-improvement strategies, intellectual goals.

My Goals:
(What I know I must Address About My Mental Health:)

_____

_____

MY LEVEL 4 INDEX CARD STATEMENTS:

(Reminder: Write ONE statement per card!)

"I am a person who keeps a journal."

Spend ten minutes at a time practicing one of these behaviors:

- Do an online search for journal prompts.
- Write a letter to your younger self.
- Write a letter to your older self.
- Write a letter to someone important to you, but don't send it.
- Write a letter to your children, or to your future children, or to the children you might have had if you'd had children.

My Ideas for Ten Minute Journal Sessions:

_____

_____

"I am a person who examines my thoughts."

Spend ten minutes at a time practicing one of these behaviors:

- Do an internet search about distorted thinking.
- Watch a video about logic.

- Write down an opinion you hold about someone. Why would that opinion seem true? Write it down. Now write why that seems true. Now write why that seems true. Have you uncovered a totally logical belief, or can you change your opinion a little?
- Examine how often you talk about yourself.

My Ideas for Ten Minutes to Check My Thinking:

_____

_____

"I am a person who seeks help."

Spend ten minutes at a time practicing one of these behaviors:

- Ask for help with household chores.
- Ask for help with a task at work. You might have allies you didn't even know existed!
- Ask for help to deal with something emotionally.
- Research local therapists just in case you'd like to call one of them.
- Do an internet search for forums and websites which cater to people who have quit smoking.

My Ideas for Ten-Minute Actions to Lighten My Burden:

_____

_____

"I am a person who practices gratitude."

Spend ten minutes at a time practicing one of these behaviors:

- Get your journal and write everything you are thankful for during a full ten-minute timeframe. Set a timer, and try to write for the entire ten minutes.
- Send a Thank-you note to someone who did something helpful to you.
- Look through the photos on your phone, if you have any photos of people who mean a lot to you.
- Start a scrapbook.
- Call a friend and tell them you missed them.
- Call a family member and tell them how glad you are to be related.

My Ideas for a Ten-Minute Gratitude Break:

_____

_____

"I am a person who practices kindness and service."

Spend ten minutes at a time practicing one of these behaviors:

- Research volunteer opportunities in your area.
- Brew a fresh pot of coffee for the office.
- Ask someone how their day is going, and listen to all of their response.
- Think about it: If anyone around you needed a helping hand, would they know that they could call you? Why or why not? What are you going to do about it?

My Ideas for Ten-Minute Acts of Kindness:

_____

_____

"I am a person who seeks laughter."

Spend ten minutes at a time practicing one of these behaviors:

- Subscribe to a daily joke message or email.
- Write a few jokes on an index card, memorize them and tell them to others.
- Find a local comedy club.
- Watch stand-up comedy videos.

- Watch a comedy movie.
- Invite a friend to come and watch a comedy movie with you.
- Call someone who has a great sense of humor, in your opinion.

My Ideas for Ten-Minute Laugh Breaks:

_____

_____

"I am a person with a healthy relationship to shame."
Spend ten minutes at a time practicing one of these behaviors:

- Research shame.
- Find resources (books, articles) about healthy shame.
- Look up a workbook for building self-esteem.
- Watch a compilation of funny videos and think about how awkward we all are at times.

My Ideas for Ten Minutes of Getting Real:

_____

_____

"I am a person who studies positivity."

Spend ten minutes at a time practicing one of these behaviors:

- Research positivity in different cultures and religions.
- Find quotes about happiness.
- Listen to music that makes you want to dance.
- Find someone close to you and choose something to compliment them on.
- Tell someone around you that they are doing a great job.
- Send someone an encouraging note.

My Ideas for a Ten-Minute Positivity Boost:

_____

_____

"I am a person who practices learned optimism."

Spend ten minutes at a time practicing one of these behaviors:

- Research books on learned optimism.
- Think about your dream job.
- Think about your dream house.
- Go to an open house and look around.

- Test-drive a luxury car, just for fun.
- Work on a vision board.

My Ideas for Ten Minutes of Optimism:

_____

_____

"I am a person who evaluates the influences in my life."
Spend ten minutes at a time practicing one of these
behaviors:

- Make a list of everything you watch on television.
  Ask yourself if they are positively or negatively
  influencing your day.
- Go through all your music and eliminate anything
  that isn't positive to your recovery.
- Go through your social media and block any
  accounts that tempt you to compare or make you
  feel inadequate.
- Go through your contacts and eliminate information
  for contacts which do not contribute to your
  positivity.

My Ideas for Ten-Minute Clean-Ups:

_____

_____

"I am a person who decides not to remain a victim."

Spend ten minutes at a time practicing one of these behaviors:

- Make a list of everything you have survived in your life.
- Wrap yourself in a cozy blanket and treat yourself like a grieving child for ten minutes.
- Look in the mirror and appreciate everything you've been through.
- Think about how your experiences have made you into who you are today.
- Write about which experiences you are going to put in your past.

My Ideas for Ten Minutes of Empowerment:

_____

_____

"I am a person who practices forgiveness."

Spend ten minutes at a time practicing one of these behaviors:

- Think about people who have wronged you.
- Think about people whom you have wronged.

- Decide to forgive someone who has wronged you.
- Write a letter of forgiveness to someone or something, and keep it in your journal instead of sending it.
- Decide to forgive yourself for something.

My Ideas for Ten-Minute Peace Treaties:

_____

_____

"I am a person who practices self-improvement."

Spend ten minutes at a time practicing one of these behaviors:

- Sign up for a cooking class.
- Sign up for a martial arts class.
- Do a crossword puzzle.
- Sign up for a class at your closest university.
- Browse online courses.

My Ideas for Ten-Minute Ninja Training:

_____

_____

Congratulations!

Congratulations for successfully integrating Level 4 into your new life as a non-smoker! Isn't it amazing how using time for these things instead of smoking cigarettes can be so transformative and real? I hope you have uncovered more beautiful things to explore.

What kind of person do you want to be in your approach to mental health? Can you describe your thoughts and needs in order to add more Level 4 cards?

Write your statements here for future cards:

I am a person who:_____.

I am a person who:_____.

I am a person who:_____.

I am a person who:_____.

I am a person who:_____.

I am a person who:_____.

I am a person who:_____.

I am a person who:_____.

I am a person who:_____.

I am a person who:_____.

I am a person who:_____.

I am a person who:_____.

My Card Pile

Here are all the cards you should have in your card pile:

Level 1: Acceptance

Level 2: Achieving Authentic Rest

Level 3: Physical

Level 4: Mental

Keep cycling through them!

Don't forget to move a marble from one glass container to the other for every card you practice during your withdrawal symptoms.

When your glass container is full of marbles, use your rewards system plan to reward yourself!

Level 5: Social

We all know the saying "You can't give away what you don't have." It refers to the amount of love we are capable of sharing with others. I believe this saying is rooted in truth--I think it's impossible to really love someone else if you don't have any love for your own life. We might try to do it sometimes, but I've never heard of it working out. I have always witnessed this lack of balance actually create dysfunctional, codependent relationships, kind of like the relationship I had with cigarette smoking.

This really was my big reason for working on my relationships with myself and others during my recovery from smoking cigarettes. By studying, practicing, encouraging, and doing the work for a happy and healthy relationship with myself first, I soon became able to project that balance towards my relationship with others. I found that some people simply weren't good friends for me, just like cigarettes were not a good friendship for me. I let all of those influences go in peace, without hatred or grudges. It didn't derail my life or my emotions, not even for a moment.

Conversely, the relationships that remained in my life became richer and more nourishing, in both directions. I was better able to both give and receive compassion, friendship, love, intimacy, honesty, companionship, and positivity. This transformation was miraculous. Today, I have a very small circle of friends whom I consider my extended family. With this family, including the people I am related to, there is more love, trust, and overall joy than I have ever experienced in my life. Cigarette smokers are often trashed-on by society, and this experience could make anyone shy and untrusting of people. It can seem like a very cruel world out there. If this is you, I want you to consider that maybe your world could be kinder one day. Until you trust the world again, just trust my words. This work is hard, but it is so indescribably worth the effort.

I realize many of us have to deal with unkind people in an unkind world. It might be difficult to approach work in the social category because often it makes us feel vulnerable. If you have endured a life of torment up to this point, full of villains or cruelty, please know that I am thinking of you and praying for you as I write this. I wish you hadn't had those experiences. I'm sure there are things that happened to you which were not fair, and that you absolutely did not deserve at all. No one deserves cruelty. I hope you'll continue to show the strength and energy you obviously have by putting some good love towards yourself. You do not have to wait to be loved by people who don't have the skills to love themselves. You *do* deserve love, and to be loved. It's out there. Don't give up on it.

Level Goals:

Quality time with myself, quality time with friends and family, gratitude, "dating myself," self care, cultivating a love for my own life, feeling happy about being alive.

My Goals:

(What I Must Do For Healthy Relationships With Myself and Others:)

_____

_____

MY LEVEL 5 INDEX CARD STATEMENTS:

(Reminder: Write ONE statement per card!)

"I am a person who has a great relationship with myself."
Spend ten minutes at a time practicing one of these
behaviors:

- Look in the mirror and think compassionate
  thoughts about yourself on purpose.
- Eat a meal that you know is healthy for you.
- Brush your teeth and care for your oral health.
- Move to/live in a place that is safe physically.
- Move to/live in a place that is safe emotionally.
- Move to/live in a place that is safe psychologically.
- Research what these different kinds of "safety"
  mean.
- Dress in a way that makes you respect yourself.

My Ideas for Ten-Minute Self Love:

_____

_____

"I am a person who spends quality time with friends."
Spend ten minutes at a time practicing one of these
behaviors:

- Ask a friend about the town they were born in.
- Make a list of questions you've always wanted to
  ask your friends.

- Research online about questions which bring people closer.
- Shop for birthday cards for your friends.
- Check your calendar and make sure your friends' birthdays are entered.
- Call them to talk about a special day they have coming up.
- Go out for coffee.
- Go see a movie.

My Ideas for Ten-Minute Friendship Builders:

_____

_____

"I am a person who is very strict with my use of social media."

Spend ten minutes at a time practicing one of these behaviors:

- Unfollow any "drama" contacts in your social media.
- Unfollow any contacts who use foul language.
- Unfollow any contacts who post inappropriate photos.
- Remove photos which are older than three years.
- Remove contacts with whom you haven't actually spoken in three years.

- Have a "bedtime" for your social media (Example: no more social media after 9:00 PM)
- Hire someone to handle your business/professional social media so you don't have to.

My Ideas for Respectable Social Media Breaks:

_____

_____

"I am a person who practices awareness of my body language."

Spend ten minutes at a time practicing one of these behaviors:

- Read a book about body language.
- Practice different postures from what you have learned.
- Observe the body language of the next person who speaks with you.
- Observe your own body language in your next conversation with someone else.
- Ask yourself: "What do I want my body language to consistently convey? Warmth? Professionalism?"

My Ideas for Ten-Minute Body Language Practice Sessions:

_____

_____

"I am a person who calls."

Spend ten minutes at a time practicing one of these behaviors:

- Update the contacts in your phone or address book.
- Call someone whom you've been meaning to call for a while.
- Have a conversation that begins with: "I only have ten minutes, but I just wanted to call since I was thinking of you today."
- Pick one text message you were going to send today and make a call instead.
- Call a family member you haven't spoken with in a while.

My Ideas for Ten-Minute Phone Call Breaks:

_____

_____

"I am a person who learns about small talk."

Spend ten minutes at a time practicing one of these behaviors:

- Take yourself out to eat and practice small talk with the server at your restaurant.
- Read a book about how to talk to anyone.
- Watch videos about small talk.
- Ask someone how their day is going.

My Ideas for Ten-Minute Small Talk Skill-Building:

_____

_____

"I am a person who invites others."

Spend ten minutes at a time practicing one of these behaviors:

- Plan a fun outing.
- Invite a friend to your outing.
- Invite a family member to your outing.
- Invite someone out to coffee with you.
- Browse recipes you can use to host dinner at your place.
- Ask a colleague out to lunch.

My Ten-Minute Ideas for Things I Can Plan With Others;

_____

_____

"I am a person who spends time alone."

Spend ten minutes at a time practicing one of these behaviors:

- Study the difference between being alone and being lonely.
- Go to a movie by yourself.
- Go to a coffee by yourself.
- Go to a dinner by yourself.
- Go somewhere quiet and sit peacefully.
- Go for a walk by yourself.
- Spend ten minutes planning a solo vacation.

My Ideas for Ten Minutes of Alone Time:

_____

_____

Only you can build a relationship with yourself. You are the only person who can teach yourself that you are loveable, worthwhile, and that you matter, and your life matters. Love yourself, and love your life; they are gifts you have been given! *Enjoy them*! Create more cards to help you craft a loving relationship with yourself. Use more cards to help you practice extending the love you find toward other people.

Write your statements here for future cards:

I am a person who:_____.

I am a person who:_____.

I am a person who:_____.

I am a person who:_____.

I am a person who:_____.

I am a person who:_____.

I am a person who:_____.

I am a person who:_____.

I am a person who:_____.

I am a person who:_____.

I am a person who:_____.

I am a person who:_____.

Congratulations!

Congratulations on integrating Level 5 cards into your quit program! I truly hope you have started to discover that you are a curious, wonderful, miraculous, magnificent creature, and that you are completely deserving of this health you are building in your life.

My Card Pile

Here are all the cards you should have in your card pile:

Level 1: Acceptance

Level 2: Achieving Authentic Rest

Level 3: Physical

Level 4: Mental

Level 5: Social

Keep cycling through them!

Don't forget to move a marble from one glass container to the other for every card you practice during your withdrawal symptoms.

When your glass container is full of marbles, use your rewards system plan to reward yourself!

Level 6: Professional

Your professional life fits in with your transition to the life of a non-smoker, but not in the way you might think. Some people remember a time when it was socially acceptable to smoke in the middle of the office, while others hold a more recent view of smoking cigarettes as inconsiderate and unprofessional.

I don't care about either of those perspectives. Seriously.

I don't care about them because honestly, people are going to find something to talk about at the office. If it isn't smoking cigarettes, it will certainly be something else for the gossip mill. Forget about them.

Your professional life fits in with your transition to life as a non-smoker because it is all to do with your life's work. Recovering is a big part of that. I found a huge benefit in thinking about my "ideal job" during my recovery for several reasons. Mostly, though, thinking about my career at this stage helped me understand that this recovery time was only a brief time in my life. Thinking about my professional goals helped me keep that sense that this recovery time was not the way things would be forever. There would be other adventures to take, other mountains to climb.

Besides, it's awfully hard to reach for your dreams until you've given yourself the time to figure out what those dreams actually are.

But I'm Retired/I'm Disabled/I'm a House Spouse

If you've completed your big career goals and you've gotten to retire, first of all LUCKY YOU, and secondly, why not make some goals about how to give back to your community? Can you start a non-profit, or volunteer? Can you do some networking and establish yourself as a mentor for professionals who are just starting out?

If you are disabled or home with an illness, you are still loveable and worthwhile. You still have tons that you can contribute to the world. Don't forget the merit of simply being home and praying for others. Imagine all the souls out there with no one to pray for them except you. See? The world needs you! There's tons to do!

And if you are a House Spouse, I want you to know first and foremost that I think any time people spend with their homes and families is a phenomenal value. It might even be priceless! Why not give yourself some goals for the kind of role you want to have in your family? If you are helping create your home, you are a Homemaker. That's a real title of a role to have! Explore accordingly.

Level Goals:

To push the limits of my capabilities, to be well-rounded and informed in my field, to be a positive contributor to the world around me.

My Goals:

(What I Must Do For My Dream Work:)

_____

_____

MY LEVEL 6 INDEX CARD STATEMENTS:

(Reminder: Write ONE statement per card!)

"I am a person with a great resume."

Spend ten minutes at a time practicing one of these behaviors:

- Find a template for your new resume.
- Update the references section of your resume.
- Update the experience section of your resume.
- Research different resumes and how they are structured.

My Ideas for Ten-Minute Resume Workshops:

_____

_____

"I am a person who knows about my financial goals."

Spend ten minutes at a time practicing one of these behaviors:

- Work on a budget.
- Make a list of things you'd like to buy.
- Research savings plans.
- Read books about economics.
- Watch videos about investing.

My Ideas for Working on Wealth:

_____

_____

"I am a person who dresses the part."

Spend ten minutes at a time practicing one of these behaviors:

- Learn different ways to tie a necktie (regardless of your gender).
- Practice different ways of tying a necktie.
- Research appropriate costuming for various professions.
- Browse three-piece suits.

My Ideas for Suiting-Up in Ten Minutes:

_____

_____

"I am a person with great skills."

Spend ten minutes at a time practicing one of these behaviors:

- Think about people you admire.
- Write down what qualities you admire most.

- Write in your journal about a superpower you'd like and how you would use it.
- Look for places where you could learn skills you've always wanted to have.
- Think about what makes you different and interesting.

My Ideas for Ten-Minute Super Skill-sets:

_____

_____

"I am a person who knows a lot about my industry."
Spend ten minutes at a time practicing one of these behaviors:
- Use a search engine to read news about your industry.
- Write a letter to a top-performer in your industry.
- Look at training programs in your industry.
- Find conferences to attend for your industry.

My Ideas for Being at the Top of My Game:

_____

_____

"I am a person who practices confidence."

Spend ten minutes at a time practicing one of these behaviors:

- Write about what confidence means to you.
- Practice different stances in the mirror.
- Go for a walk and practice walking with your head held high.
- Spend ten minutes doing everything standing/sitting up straight.

My Ideas for Ten-Minute Confidence Boosters:

_____

_____

"I am a person who appreciates others."

Spend ten minutes at a time practicing one of these behaviors:

- Search for people doing things you can admire.
- Send a thank-you note.
- Send a note of appreciation for work well done.
- Remember important dates for your colleagues.
- Include colleagues in your plans for attending conferences and lectures.
- Read anything by Dale Carnegie.

My Ideas for Being a Ten-Minute Team Player:

_____

_____

"I am a person who does what I say I will do."

Spend ten minutes at a time practicing one of these behaviors:

- Look up "reliability" in a dictionary.
- Get a planner.
- Organize your appointments.
- Create appointments for events and time with people.
- Prepare notes, papers, etc. for future meetings.

My Ideas for Ten-Minute Reliability Skills:

_____

_____

"I am a person who studies success."

Spend ten minutes at a time practicing one of these behaviors:

- Read books about habits.
- Read books about time management.

- Read books by interesting people.
- Read books by people who are more successful than you.

My Ideas for Ten-Minute Success Studies:

_____

_____

"I am a person who is finding my 'dream job.'"
Spend ten minutes at a time practicing one of these behaviors:
- Make a list of your talents.
- Make a list of your strengths.
- Make a list of your weaknesses.
- Think about the job you wanted when you were 5 years old.
- Think about how you might be using your time right now, if you could be doing anything.

My Ideas for Ten Minutes of Planning my Dream:

_____

_____

My hope is that these things have gotten you thinking about yourself as a worthwhile professional in your field, whatever field that may be. Whatever happens during your recovery time from nicotine, I hope that it becomes transformative for your confidence levels, and your own understanding of what you're capable of.

Congratulations!

You've successfully re-vamped your recovery to also include refreshing your professional skills! Are you starting to feel confident? Accomplished? Here's why this is so important:

Chances are, quitting cigarettes once seemed like something that was impossible for you to figure out how to do, due to your circumstances or current set of skills. With your newfound confidence and skills, does it still seem like an impossible task? Of course not! You are a powerful creature. Do you really think you could accept an excuse from yourself to *not* do your best in your recovery? No way! You are on your path, and you are going to rock it.

You've got this.

Write your statements here for future cards:

I am a person who:_____.

I am a person who:_____.

I am a person who:_____.

I am a person who:_____.

I am a person who:_____.

I am a person who:_____.

I am a person who:_____.

I am a person who:_____.

I am a person who:_____.

I am a person who:_____.

I am a person who:_____.

I am a person who:_____.

My Card Pile

Here are all the cards you should have in your card pile:

Level 1: Acceptance

Level 2: Achieving Authentic Rest

Level 3: Physical

Level 4: Mental

Level 5: Social

Level 6: Professional

Keep cycling through them!

Don't forget to move a marble from one glass container to the other for every card you practice during your withdrawal symptoms.

When your glass container is full of marbles, use your rewards system plan to reward yourself!

Level 7: Creative

The big thing going on around the world right now is consumerism. Tell anyone you are off to do some "retail therapy," and it's pretty likely that they'll know exactly what you're talking about.

I would like to propose a bit of a counter-cultural approach to stress relief: Instead of going out and buying something to alleviate your stress, work on your creative skills instead!

Not only is it common knowledge that creativity relieves stress, it's also well-known that having a creative outlet leads to better problem-solving, gives a sense of play (which we adults still need to do!), and helps us feel accomplished and productive. We are the wonderful human race. We're makers. We're tinkers. We're doers, doing things.

Since you have these wonderful ten-minute blocks during your waves of withdrawal symptoms, why not use them to develop your creative skills?

Level Goals:

To expand my creative skills, to learn about problem-solving, to expose myself to rich cultural arts, to enjoy the fine things in the world around me.

My Goals:

(What I Must Do For My Creativity:)

_____

_____

MY LEVEL 7 INDEX CARD STATEMENTS:

(Reminder: Write ONE statement per card!)

"I am a person who goes after the creative pursuits I've always dreamed about."

Spend ten minutes at a time practicing one of these behaviors:

- Start writing a screenplay.
- Write a poem about your day.
- Write your own book about quitting smoking.
- Learn to paint.
- Learn to draw.

- Learn to knit.
- Learn to decorate a cake.
- Learn to cook.
- Learn an instrument.

My Ideas for Things I've Always Wanted to Learn to Do:

_____

_____

"I am a person who exposes myself to new ideas."
Spend ten minutes at a time practicing one of these
behaviors:

- Attend a political rally of a viewpoint you disagree
  with, strictly as an observer.
- Attend a church service at a place you've never
  been to.
- Attend a religious service for a religion you don't
  belong to.
- Plan a trip to a different country.
- Study cultural traditions of people from different
  countries than you.

My Ideas to Broaden My Horizons:

_____

_____

"I am a person who meets new people."

Spend ten minutes at a time practicing one of these behaviors:

- Join a club for Public Speaking.
- Join a yoga class.
- Join a walking/knitting/book club.
- Attend church once a week.
- If you're single, attend a speed-dating night with the idea of making friends.

My Ideas for Meeting New People:

_____

_____

"I am a person who learns about art."

Spend ten minutes at a time practicing one of these behaviors:

- Browse art books at the bookstore.
- Attend a university art gallery.
- Attend a commercial art gallery.
- Do an internet search of arts and culture.
- Make a mission for yourself to decide who your favorite fine artist is.
- Try to recreate a famous painting.
- Make an original painting.

- Make an original sculpture.
- Make an original drawing.
- Make an original film.

My Ideas for A Ten-Minute Art Appreciation Class:

_____

_____

"I am a person who learns about architecture."

Spend ten minutes at a time practicing one of these behaviors:

- Read a book about architecture.
- Walk around and observe the architecture of your location. Record your impressions in your journal.
- Sketch local buildings you find beautiful.
- Sketch local buildings you find atrocious.
- Travel to a different city and look at the architecture.
- Do an internet search with the mission of discovering your favorite architect.
- Sketch a building, house, or idea for furniture.

My Ideas for "Building" An Appreciation for Architecture:

_____

_____

"I am a person who learns about philosophy."

Spend ten minutes at a time practicing one of these behaviors:

- Watch videos about philosophy.
- Write down your worldview.
- Read books about philosophers.
- Research modern philosophers.
- Attend a talk about a philosopher you agree with.
- Attend a talk about a philosopher you disagree with.

My Ideas for Ten-Minute Philosophy Breaks:

_____

_____

"I am a person who participates in The Arts."

Spend ten minutes at a time practicing one of these behaviors:

- Get tickets for a ballet.
- Get tickets for a symphony concert.
- Get tickets for a film festival.
- Attempt to create a short film.
- Attend a high school musical production.
- Attend a university theater production.

- Watch videos online from famous opera houses.

My Ideas for Ten-Minute Arts and Culture Explorations:

_____

_____

Arts and Culture don't belong to just one group of people. They belong to us all. They are our heritage and ours to enjoy. They are beautiful (hopefully), and inspiring. This is a great time to congratulate yourself for making it this far. Did you ever dream that you could attend a symphony concert without worrying about how many hours it might take so you could have a cigarette? There are millions of people who have been in those auditorium seats, soaking up the finer things while you've been enslaved outside. Not any more! Come and join the finest parts of civilization. You've *always* had a right to be here. You've *always* had it in you to contribute something beautiful and good to the rest of the world. Now that you are a non-smoker, you are free to give to the rest of the world, from your whole heart.

Congratulations!

You've done a ton of work to start integrating creative pursuits into your recovery. Now that you are getting your health in order, you can start dreaming dreams and having ideas you never thought were possible before.

What are your other ideas for creative pursuits? What kinds of things have you always wanted to do? Describe yourself *to* yourself, outlining the kind of creative mind you are, or the kind of creative person you are on your way to becoming!

Write your statements here for future cards:

I am a person who:_____.

I am a person who:_____.

I am a person who:_____.

I am a person who:_____.

I am a person who:_____.

I am a person who:_____.

I am a person who:_____.

I am a person who:_____.

I am a person who:_____.

I am a person who:_____.

I am a person who:_____.

I am a person who:_____.

My Card Pile

Here are all the cards you should have in your card pile:

Level 1: Acceptance

Level 2: Achieving Authentic Rest

Level 3: Physical

Level 4: Mental

Level 5: Social

Level 6: Professional

Level 7: Creative

Keep cycling through them!

Don't forget to move a marble from one glass container to the other for every card you practice during your withdrawal symptoms.

When your glass container is full of marbles, use your rewards system plan to reward yourself!

Level 8: Spiritual

There is nothing in this world quite like spiritual healing. Literally! Contemplating the super-natural world helps us see ourselves within a bigger picture. It would be very fair to argue that the previous chapters sort of helped me get my business in order so that I could begin the task of working on my identity beyond the physical and mental aspects of life.

For me, this chapter was all about thinking about my soul. What is good and healthy for the soul? What helps the soul grow and develop?

I found lots of answers, and I did rekindle a relationship with God, which was something I did not expect at all while recovering from nicotine. (Trust me, I was about as far away from that as they come.) This chapter is written from a Christian perspective, since that's the way I relate to this type of work.

I don't know what sort of paths lay ahead for you to explore as you find time to redirect your nicotine recovery toward ways that feed and nourish your soul. I certainly won't pretend to know what is best for your soul in this regard.

However, as someone who has done a little exploring in this area, I will share this for you to contemplate going forward: If a person as ridiculous and imperfect as I am can find a God who extends her such mercy and love, then there is most certainly that same amount of love (or more!) waiting for you. Don't miss out.

Level Goals:

Healing and nourishing my soul through this recovery process and beyond, growing close in my relationship to God.

My Goals:

(What I Know I Must Do For My Spiritual Health:)

_____

_____

MY LEVEL 8 INDEX CARD STATEMENTS:

(Reminder: Write ONE statement per card!)

"I am a person who prays."

Spend ten minutes at a time practicing one of these behaviors:

- Tell God about your day.
- Tell God "Hi."
- Write a letter containing all the questions you want to ask God.
- Learn the Jesus Prayer.
- Listen to a Requiem.
- Listen to Gregorian Chants.
- Start a journal just for prayer requests.

My Ideas for Spending Ten Minutes In Prayer:

_____

_____

"I am a person who studies belief systems."

Spend ten minutes at a time practicing one of these behaviors:

- Watch videos about a religion different from yours/a religion you know nothing about.
- Watch videos about a religion you admire.
- Write an email to someone who has a different faith than you, and ask them if they will tell you why their faith is so special to them.
- Read a book about belief systems around the world.
- Take a theology class.

My Ideas to Broaden my Religious Vocabulary:

_____

_____

"I am a person who knows what I believe."

Spend ten minutes at a time practicing one of these behaviors:

- Write your own statement of faith.
- Write about what your soul needs to heal from.
- Take a walk and think about your beliefs.
- Think about how you'd describe your beliefs to someone else.

My Ideas for Ten Minute Belief Development Sessions:

_____

_____

"I am a person with a relationship with God."
Spend ten minutes at a time practicing one of these behaviors:

- Listen to music that makes you feel close to a Higher Power.
- Take a nature walk.
- Take ten minutes to "hang out" with God.
- Take a drive and feel that connection within you.

My Ideas for Connecting with God:

_____

_____

"I am a person who practices the Works of Mercy."
Spend ten minutes at a time practicing one of these behaviors:

- Read about the Works of Mercy described by Jesus Christ.
- Think: What does it mean to feed the hungry?
- Think: What does it mean to shelter the homeless?

- Think: What does it mean to clothe the naked?
- Think: What does it mean to visit the sick?
- Think: What does it mean to bear wrongs patiently?

My Ideas for Ten Minute Mercy Research:

_____

_____

"I am a person who prays the Rosary."

Spend ten minutes at a time practicing one of these behaviors:

- Learn how to make a Rosary chain.
- Look up the Mysteries of the Rosary.
- Learn how to pray a Rosary prayer.
- Research the history of the Rosary prayer.

My Ideas for Ten Minutes of Rosary Research:

_____

_____

"I am a person who reads more about my faith."

Spend ten minutes at a time practicing one of these behaviors:

- Read a holy book, if my faith has one.
- Research great orators/philosophers in my faith.

- Read books and essays by theologians.
- Look up communities of like-minded people.

My Ideas to Learn More About my Faith:

_____

_____

"I am a person who takes time to be alone with God."
Spend ten minutes at a time practicing one of these behaviors:

- Clear my planner at consistent times for availability to God.
- Take a walk around the block and talk to God.
- Sit in silence and listen from your soul.

My Ideas for Ten Minute Retreats:

_____

_____

"I am a person who does my best to be virtuous today."
Spend ten minutes at a time practicing one of these behaviors:

- Make a list of virtues.
- Pick a virtue to contemplate.
- Make a plan for growing in virtue.

- Research wiser/more educated perspectives on virtues.

My Ideas for Ten Minute Training for A Virtuous Heart:

_____

_____

"I am a person who makes reparations."

Spend ten minutes at a time practicing one of these behaviors:

- Tell God about something you messed up with.
- Ask for forgiveness from God for something you messed up with.
- Make a plan to repair your relationship to God in honor of the mercy you've been given.
- Tell someone in your life about something you messed up with towards them.
- Ask for forgiveness from that person for something you messed up with towards them.
- Make a plan to repair your relationship with that person in honor of the mercy you've been given.

My Ideas to Work On Making Things Better:

_____

_____

Like I said before, I have no idea what is ahead for you, waiting to nurture and heal your soul. What I do know is that we all need this type of spiritual healing in our lives--especially those of us who are recovering from any sort of addiction, illness, or any sort of malaise of the soul. Again, I say: If someone like me can find healing here, there is most assuredly health, mercy, and love to be found for you.

For what it's worth, I'm praying for you, and I hope you'll pray for me too.

Congratulations!

Congratulations on taking the brave and wonderful step to add spiritual growth and healing to your recovery from nicotine!

Write your statements here for future cards:

I am a person who:_____.

I am a person who:_____.

I am a person who:_____.

I am a person who:_____.

I am a person who:_____.

I am a person who:_____.

I am a person who:_____.

I am a person who:_____.

I am a person who:_____.

I am a person who:_____.

I am a person who:_____.

I am a person who:_____.

My Card Pile

Here are all the cards you should have in your card pile:

Level 1: Acceptance

Level 2: Achieving Authentic Rest

Level 3: Physical

Level 4: Mental

Level 5: Social

Level 6: Professional

Level 7: Creative

Level 8: Spiritual

Keep cycling through them!

Don't forget to move a marble from one glass container to the other for every card you practice during your withdrawal symptoms.

When your glass container is full of marbles, use your rewards system plan to reward yourself!

Level 9: Celebrating

I'd like to point this out: If you have made it this far, and have followed-along chapter by chapter, you have developed a system for yourself which takes the old waves of addiction, shame, and withdrawal and transforms them into new and beautiful ways of existing on peaceful, physical, mental, social, professional, creative, and spiritual levels.

Everything has all added up to this.

If you haven't done so yet, now is a great time to finally get to look back on your quit experience so far. You have likely been busy doing so very many things, in tons of different areas of your life. *None of these many many things had anything to do with smoking cigarettes.* By now, you should feel that you have proven to yourself that you CAN do this, and you ARE transitioning to a rich, full, beautiful life as a non-smoker.

This chapter is all about ideas for celebrating our hard work, and our freedom from nicotine!

Our culture has a tendency to give shame to people who are genuinely enjoying their lives, and this is no surprise. This focus on shame and comparison is prevalent in today's society. It can make everyday enjoyment seem like something we aren't "allowed" to do, which is why I am spending a chapter on it.

I believe 100% that you should absolutely continue to use the marbles and your reward system, even for practicing your Celebration cards. Why? *Because it is good for your brain to learn this truth: That life is valuable, life is intricate and beautiful, and* **YOUR life is absolutely worth living.**

Level Goals:

Loving, Enjoying, and Celebrating the simple fact that I get to be alive and free!

My Goals:

(What I Know I Must Do To Celebrate Being Alive:)

_____

_____

MY LEVEL 9 INDEX CARD STATEMENTS:

(Reminder: Write ONE statement per card!)

"I am a person who celebrates myself."

Spend ten minutes at a time practicing one of these behaviors:

- Buy yourself a cupcake.
- Buy yourself a coffee from the best place in town.
- Rent your favorite movie.
- Cook your favorite meal.
- Take yourself on a date.
- Take yourself to a concert.

- Post on social media about your progress as a non-smoker.

My Ideas for a Ten-Minute "Yay Me!" Mini Party:

_____

_____

"I am a person who celebrates with dinners."

Spend ten minutes at a time practicing one of these behaviors:

- Take yourself out to your favorite restaurant.
- Meet friends for a celebratory "Life is Good" dinner.
- Plan a dinner party at your place.
- Eat dinner by candlelight.
- Eat dinner on fine china

My Ideas for Moments of La Dolce Vita:

_____

_____

"I am a person who celebrates with photography."

Spend ten minutes at a time practicing one of these behaviors:

- Set up portraits with a local photographer.
- Go to a photo booth with your significant other.

- Go on a photography adventure by yourself.
- Go on a photography adventure with someone special to you.
- Print out a special photo and buy a fancy frame for it.

My Ideas for Ten Minute Eye Candy:

_____

_____

"I am a person who celebrates with greeting cards."
Spend ten minutes at a time practicing one of these behaviors:

- Go look through the humor greeting card section at the store.
- Buy cards for all the children in your family.
- Buy a greeting card for your spouse to say how much you love and appreciate them.
- Look up a way to send greeting cards to soldiers.

My Ideas for Ten Minute Correspondence Breaks:

_____

_____

"I am a person who creates regular opportunities to feel joy."

Spend ten minutes at a time practicing one of these behaviors:

- Plan a birthday surprise for someone else.
- Look up local theater productions and plan your next theater night.
- Look up your favorite band and plan your next concert visit.
- Go out to dinner and dancing this weekend.

My Ideas to Let My Hair Down:

_____

_____

"I am a person who sees myself as a non-smoker."

Spend ten minutes at a time practicing one of these behaviors:

- Think about the best thing that happened to you because of becoming a non-smoker.
- Think about what advice you would give someone else who was about to become a non-smoker.
- Create a poster of any goals or visions you have discovered for your life since becoming a non-smoker.

My Ideas to Reaffirm my Non-Smoking Identity:

_____

_____

Write your statements here for future cards:

I am a person who:_____.

I am a person who:_____.

I am a person who:_____.

I am a person who:_____.

I am a person who:_____.

I am a person who:_____.

I am a person who:_____.

I am a person who:_____.

I am a person who:_____.

I am a person who:_____.

I am a person who:_____.

I am a person who:_____.

Congratulations!

Oh how I wish I could hug you right this very moment! Since I can't hug you, I'll do something else.

I want to thank you.

Thank you for standing-up for yourself. Thank you for loving your life. Thank you for fighting for your freedom from nicotine. Thank you for developing your identity. Thank you for your hard work. Thank you for feeling the sacrifice that comes along with changing your life. Thank you for praying. Thank you for healing. Thank you for having faith. Thank you for thinking about creative solutions to problems. Thank you for enjoying yourself. Thank you for trying out this game. Thank you for developing your own way of doing things.

Thank you for being you. There's no one else in the whole world who could have done it.

My Card Pile

Here are all the cards you should have in your card pile:

Level 1: Acceptance

Level 2: Achieving Authentic Rest

Level 3: Physical

Level 4: Mental

Level 5: Social

Level 6: Professional

Level 7: Creative

Level 8: Spiritual

Level 9: Celebrating

Keep cycling through them!

Don't forget to move a marble from one glass container to the other for every card you practice during your withdrawal symptoms.

When your glass container is full of marbles, use your rewards system plan to reward yourself!

Continuing Success, Part 1: Reminders About Relapse

My greatest fear before I quit was: What if I start smoking again? I had this fear, and it was gut-wrenching, before I even started my quit recovery. I think I was so scared of failing, it actually prevented me from starting my quit recovery sooner.

Here are some suggestions for things to think about in regards to relapsing, especially if you are scared of failing like I was.

Reminder #1

You've only been writing "I am a person who…" statements about a thousand times so far in this book. You know why? Because you are a person. You are not a superhero, and you are not a god...and don't believe anyone who would tell you otherwise. I get irked by these "self-help" gurus who try to convince people they have their own gods within them. Like a DIY-Deity. Nope, you're no god, my friend. You are a human person, and if you have made a mistake, you have made a mistake. Just own it.

Reminder #2

It's not over 'till you give up. If you are willing to try again, then you haven't given up. Don't throw away anything just yet.

Reminder #3

You need to figure out what influenced your failure. Was it the way you approached a stressful situation? Hey, life happens. We can't blame the situation itself for being stressful--that's just an attempt to find an excuse. We can only pay attention to how we handled a stressful situation, and accept our actions as best as we can. Was it the way you approached a situation with a person? Was it a matter of not planning your day well enough? What was it that caused you to fail this time?

Reminder #4

Whatever it was that influenced your failure, stop doing it! Plan around it, take a break from a lousy friend, set better boundaries, use your planner, make sure you're eating and sleeping well, get some exercise, and commit to removing toxicity from your life so that you can continue to recover.

Reminder #5

YES you are recovering, even during relapse, IF you keep approaching it as a learning experience!

Reminder #6

Go back to your cards! Keep playing them, and add more based on what you have learned from this experience. You are valuable and worthy of health.

Reminder #7

Get help if you need to! You don't have to do this alone. Don't be alone. Get the help of a professional to give you more tools.

Reminder #8

Stay positive! You are already never going to be a slave to nicotine again. You've already won that, because you decided to try this out in the first place. You've already decided you deserve something better. The rest is just building habits, that's all, and that's exactly what you're doing! Stay positive, and get the job done!

Continuing Success, Part 2: Ready to Lead

This is probably the biggest secret to success in this book. It combines everything I have written about in the previous chapters. This secret continues to fuel my life and infuse it with constant inspiration, even now that I have transitioned to life as a non-smoker.

Here are the premises behind the big secret. They are incredibly simple. Here they are:

1.) Life is full of changes.
2.) You are a human person.
3.) You are subject to the changes of life.
4.) Quitting smoking was a huge life change.

Freeing your identity from nicotine was a huge change--one that had effects in every area of your life. Hopefully this book has helped you devise a system for yourself that helped you ride the waves of change during your nicotine recovery.

Ready for the big secret? Here it is:

You can use this system for all of life's changes! Not just the hard ones, but the happy changes too!

We all must find our way in the world, and our way through time, through health, through sorrow, through joy, through happiness, through grief, and through this whole lifetime. We all must find a way to create meaning for ourselves in what we have learned. We all have to find ourselves, no matter which circumstances we find ourselves in.

Now you have a real tool to accomplish this.

Life Changes

Here are just a few examples of some of the changes you might face in your life, and when you can bring out your index cards and your marbles to help yourself cope:

- Quitting smoking
- Moving to a new city
- Selling your old house
- Recovering from a major surgery
- Parting with a significant item, such as a car, a family heirloom, etc.
- Feelings of hopelessness or loss of identity
- You've just made a huge purchase
- During a Dark Night of the Soul
- Graduating College
- Getting a new job
- Retiring
- Getting engaged
- First year of marriage
- Starting a family
- Conflict with parent/sibling/family
- Loss of a loved one
- Social isolation
- You or your partner have been fired
- You or your partner have gotten a promotion
- New mortgage
- Friend or relative moves in

- You've made a major decision
- You've made a major accomplishment
- Your finances have changed
- You are planning a huge vacation
- You have survived an illness
- You have survived a natural disaster
- You are ready to heal from trauma

There are probably countless more circumstances when we could use these cards!

Ready to Lead

I have covered how important it is to have positive influences several times in this book. I titled this chapter "Ready to Lead" because I want to point out how accomplished you are by this point. All of your hard work is work you own, and nothing and no one can ever take that away from you. Now and forever, you are free to be wholly yourself. You are not only completely ready to be responsible for yourself and your happiness, you are also now the most perfect mortal influence and champion you could ever have for yourself.

You are the best, most positive influence you have. *You* are the difference. You've got the stuff in you.

You can certainly shine your light on other people and help them out too. I'm sure you'll be great at it! But even if you don't you will still be a beacon of balance, strength, and positivity, just by how you will live your life from this point onward. You are the example now. You're ready to lead your life in to a better, brighter new direction.

I am so, so happy for you.

Made in the USA
Columbia, SC
23 July 2019